Praise for
Mental Fitness for Tweens and Teens

"Dr. Hoy's book, *Mental Fitness for Tweens and Teens: Coach Your Child to Thrive*, brings the importance of emotional intelligence to a new level. Highly recommended for parents (and grandparents) dealing with tweens and teens."

—Robert A. Saul, MD, Author, *Conscious Parenting: Parenting: Using the Parental Awareness Threshold*

"Drawing from thirty years of experience as an educator and therapist, Dr. Hoy provides a real-world, practical approach to maintaining and supporting mental and emotional health. The book is highly readable and seems like the perfect 'manual' for parents/guardians of tweens and teens."

—David Abelson, MD, Retired Chief Executive Officer, Park Nicollet Health Services

"As a parent of two internet generation kids, and as a relational therapist, I can say that *Mental Fitness for Teens and Tweens* is right on the money. There is no more powerful tool for parenting than having a genuine connection with your child. This book gives the road map to get there if you are lost."

—Megan Kunz MA, Licensed Marriage and Family Therapist, Recipient of the Distinguished Services Award by the Minnesota Association for Marriage and Family Therapy

"Dr. Hoy combines real-life stories, research, theory, and practical assignments to create a comprehensive and engaging guide for parents of children of all ages. Now a retired school administrator of thirty-plus years, I wish this book had been available years ago. I give it my highest recommendation to all parents and guardians of children of all ages."

—Elizabeth Linares, EdS

"Over the past decade, the mental health crisis in the twelve-to-twenty-five-year-old demographic has skyrocketed. Dr. Hoy's approach to addressing this crisis at scale by training parents on how to work with their children in their early years is the best way to stem this crisis and produce healthy young adults. This book is a must-have for every parent and grandparent with a tween or teen."

—John Gabos, Founder of the Career Development Academy, PRISM Networking, and Director of Mental Health for Phi Kappa Psi Fraternity

"*Mental Fitness for Tweens and Teens* can alter lives. David has a gift of storytelling that creates the desire to lean in, listen, and learn. As a mother myself, I look forward to leveraging these concepts and steps with my child. If you have a young person in your life, this book is for you!"

—Elisha Engelen, MA, LMFT

"Mr. Hoy's new book strikes gold with practical advice grounded both in rich clinical experience and, maybe more importantly and compellingly, in the author's wisdom gathered over a lifetime of relevant experience. I feel blessed that Mr. Hoy's book will be on my shelf and in my mind whenever my teen will require me to be better than my parents had the resources to be."

—Robert Ribciuc, Mental Health and Disability Inclusion Advocate, Board/Advisory Board Member of Disability:IN and Rangam Consultants, Managing Partner of EBITDA Catalyst

"David fills a 'void' for today's families with timely insight and perspective. Authentic and caring advice for navigating difficult family relationships in the complex world we live in today."

—Michael Follese, Coach, Mentor, and Father of Four, Family Financial Advisor

Mental Fitness for Tweens and Teens:
Coach Your Child to Thrive

by David Hoy

© Copyright 2024 David Hoy PhD

ISBN 979-8-88824-195-0

All rights reserved. No part of this publication may be reproduced, stored in a retrieval system, or transmitted in any form or by any means—electronic, mechanical, photocopy, recording, or any other—except for brief quotations in printed reviews, without the prior written permission of the author.

Published by

◀ köehlerbooks™

3705 Shore Drive
Virginia Beach, VA 23455
800-435-4811
www.koehlerbooks.com

MENTAL FITNESS
FOR TWEENS AND TEENS

Coach Your Child To Thrive

David Hoy PhD

VIRGINIA BEACH
CAPE CHARLES

For my love,
Sandy.

TABLE OF CONTENTS

Introduction 1

Chapter 1:
Time Is Running Out! 5

Chapter 2:
Riding the Big Red with A Sour Taste in My Mouth 12

Chapter 3:
Mental Fitness Is Key 17

Chapter 4:
Step 1—What's Happening with Your Child? 20

Chapter 5:
Step 2—What's Happening in Your World? 27

Chapter 6:
Step 3—Understanding Your iGen's Unique World 34

Chapter 7:
Step 4—Design an Alliance 67

Chapter 8:
Step 5—Lay a Solid Foundation 77

Chapter 9:
Step 6—Infuse Emotional Intelligence Skills 96

Chapter 10:
Step 7—Set Realistic Goals and Coach Your Child to Success 132

Chapter 11
Step—8: It's Not an Event, It's a Process 142

Chapter 12:
Conclusion 145

INTRODUCTION

THE OXFORD ENGLISH Dictionary defines crisis as *"a time of intense difficulty, trouble, or danger . . . a time when a difficult or important decision must be made . . . the turning point of a disease when important changes take place, indicating either recovery or death."*

Seriously, folks, our kids are in crisis!

Our kids are more lonely, mentally ill, and prone to self-harm and suicide than ever before. Suicide is now the second leading cause of death for teens and young adults. One in four students have diagnosable mental illnesses. And that's just what's reported. Do the math. This is an astronomical number, large enough that the Centers for Disease Control (CDC) has declared it an epidemic. Emergency rooms are overflowing with struggling kids who cannot access services. Wait lists in mental health clinics are six to twelve months long. There are simply not enough mental health professionals to solve the problem, nor will there ever be.

It's hard to think of our kids as lonely when we observe them hooked to their cell phones throughout the day. And it seems counterintuitive that social media leads to social isolation. Add the pandemic, forcing more isolation, and we have experienced a 25 percent increase in depression and anxiety worldwide. Researchers report that our kids are three years behind socially and emotionally and not prepared to take on the rigors of high school, college, or employment after leaving home.

In my first book, *Getting into A Good College May Not Be as Hard as You Think*, my goal was to assist parents in preparing their children for college. In the three years since the book was published, I have become aware that I may have been putting the cart before the horse by focusing on "getting into a good college." These last three years have resulted in a deluge of social stress that has caused us as a nation to step back and reevaluate our priorities. The conversation with parents in my clinics has changed from "I want my child to get a good education and be successful" to "I just want my kid to be alive, happy, and able to take care of him/herself."

Hence, the impetus to step back and write this book—a guide for parents who want their children to be mentally fit, be equipped to take on life's challenges, and thrive no matter what path they choose. Of course, we all want our children to be cooperative in the household, succeed in school, have good friends, and find meaningful employment when they leave home, but we may be getting ahead of ourselves by focusing solely on performance or achievement. Sometimes we must take a step back and get to the root cause of our children's struggles. Therefore, I am asking you to step back, take a hard-core look at your children's mental health, and learn how to promote mental fitness.

When struggling to help your child move forward, reference my research-based, step-by-step mental fitness framework, where I coach you on how to coach your kids. The two core components are foundational skills and emotional intelligence. Foundational skills are the essential survival skills your child needs to learn before leaving the nest. These skills include time and money management, sleep hygiene, nutrition, and physical activity. Although you may know a great deal about foundational skills, the bottom line is that our kids are struggling with them. My focus on these foundational skills is not as much about teaching as it is about helping you to create sustainable structures to keep your child on track.

The heart of this book is in chapter nine, where I focus on emotional intelligence skills in great detail. Think of emotional intelligence as a mixture of social and emotional skills. Our kids need to be able to identify how they are feeling and respond in a way that benefits them. They need to be socially aware to learn how to interact effectively with others. Also, they need to develop empathy skills, not just for their own health but for the planet's health. We are aware in fields of education and psychology that individuals with emotional intelligence are happier, healthier, and more successful. I am reminded of groundbreaking work done many years ago by Dr. Dan Goleman. He did a meta-analysis, a study of many studies, to discover what set star performers in the workplace apart from others. It wasn't as much about raw intelligence as it was about having highly developed social skills. In essence, you can be a very intelligent person, but to flourish and be successful, you need to have well-developed social skills. This book is packed with practical tips and actionable assignments to help you imbue your children with emotional intelligence skills for success.

I have an extensive background in coaching, physical fitness, psychology, and education. My private counseling and psychological services business, which I founded in 1997, now has eighty-five staff members. Working with families and children is my passion and priority. Since I have been on the front lines, I have seen dramatic increases in anxiety, panic attacks, depression, and suicide rates among our children. I have been inspired to write this book to empower parents on a broad social level, not only for prevention but with tools and solutions to help children thrive.

I have written this book in a manner that I hope will be most helpful to you, using examples from research, my own experience, and anecdotal stories. I have changed names and other identifying details to maintain confidentiality as I share client experiences. Parents, this is a call to action. I know you are busy, but this is extremely important. Kids are only kids for a short period of time. By reading this book and following this process, you are demonstrating your love for and commitment to your child's mental fitness.

CHAPTER 1:

Time Is Running Out!

ONE DAY, I received a phone call from a mom who was extremely frustrated with her sixteen-year-old son, Tommy. "I feel like time is running out! I don't know what he will do after he graduates high school." She brought him into my office and sat in the lobby while I chatted with him. He was slumped over in a chair, headphones on, as I walked in. I asked him how he was doing, and he replied, "Really f . . . ing shitty!" His voice rang out so loud that it could be heard through the walls. I appreciated his authenticity and thanked him for being so honest. He explained that his parents were always yelling at him and on his case. "I wish they would just get off my back." To him, all they cared about was that he looked good and got good grades.

After listening to Tommy, I had his mom come into my office. She was wearing yoga pants and a blazer, a combination of athleticism and professionalism. She seemed like a very strong person. I asked her to give me her take on what was happening with Tommy. As she started to speak, her face became red, and tears welled in her eyes. "I don't know what to do," she said. "I feel like my kid has gone crazy in the last year." She was frustrated by his lack of motivation and poor study habits. She went on to explain how he isolated himself in his room and was often impossible to converse with. When he was in his room, with the door shut, she was never sure if he was doing homework or using his cell phone. He slept late on weekends, when he could be catching up with his schoolwork, and he often had his grades docked for handing assignments in late. "Right now, he's getting Cs and Ds in all of his classes," she said, "and I don't know how he thinks he's going to get into college with those grades!" She described his room as a disaster area and said she had been finding beer cans in his closet and "weird vaping" devices that she had never seen before. Overall, she reported feeling helpless and very worried about his future.

As I talked with Tommy's mom, she told me about a burning sensation she felt in her stomach every day. She'd been having problems sleeping and felt like she was getting a little depressed herself. Her relationship with her husband had been becoming increasingly strained as they could not figure out how to help Tommy. I had her visualize her life a year down the line, asking her to picture a twelve out of ten rating. I asked, "What would that look like?" She took a deep breath and said, "Tommy would be getting mostly As and maybe some Bs. He would have a lot of good friends and a clear plan of what he wants to do when he graduates."

"And how would your life change?" I asked. She explained how relieved she would be to know that Tommy was going to have a great future. "Tell me more," I said.

"It would be a huge weight off my shoulders, not having to worry all the time." She would be able to travel more with her husband as they reached their retirement years and hoped that she would not have to worry if Tommy was okay or not. "I think it would take the strain out of my marriage and hopefully create more intimacy in our relationship." More time for hobbies and self-care would be a dream compared to the stressful year with Tommy.

I worked with Tommy and his parents for a little over six months, and although it was challenging for all of us, the family made great strides. I worked hard to create a safe space for both Tommy and his parents to share their feelings and concerns. Tommy felt like he was being punished and controlled by his parents. As he began to trust our process, he opened up about his intense fear of failure. He was overwhelmed by the size of the classes he attended in high school. It was often so loud that he couldn't concentrate and follow lesson plans. He was afraid to ask for help because he didn't want to look stupid. With tears in his eyes, he talked about being so far behind in school that he felt there was nothing he could do to get back on track. His only forms of escape were video games, his cell phone, and social media. This was a defining moment for the family.

Initially, Tommy's parents felt like he didn't care about anything and was disrespectful and defiant. When they learned about Tommy's true feelings and fears, they became less reactive (i.e., stopped yelling) and more empathetic and accepting. When Tommy became aware that they were truly an ally in his success, he began to listen to them. Over the next few months, Tommy and his parents completed assignments to improve communication and work through conflicts and disagreements.

Sadly, the story of Tommy, his parents, his bad grades, his lack of motivation, and his struggles with mental fitness is becoming a very common scenario in my practice. And people often avoid getting help. There can be multiple contributing factors to this problem. Although it is getting better, a social stigma continues to exist around asking for and receiving professional help. Disagreements can add fuel to the fire and keep parents from getting help. One parent often sees the other as coddling, while the other is seen as too strict. Sometimes, as parents caught up in day-to-day activities, we simply don't see how much our kids are struggling. And our kids don't always have the tools to tell us what they are struggling with or what they need. Frequently, when we reach this stage with our children, we become overwhelmed. As parents trying to balance work, finances, household responsibilities, other children, aging parents, and one hundred other things, it is easy to become worn out and frustrated. Frustration can lead us to behavior that isn't always helpful for our children, such as yelling, engaging in power struggles, punishing, setting unrealistic limits, or inadvertently shaming our kids. When we cling to negative behavior patterns due to stress and frustration, we risk intensifying problems and experiencing unintended consequences. Examples of escalated problems and unintended consequences for kids include high school dropouts, poor grades, mental health struggles, drug and alcohol abuse, loss of friends, lack of motivation, damaged self-esteem, negative peer groups, and legal problems.

Parental escalated problems and consequences include high stress, depression and anxiety, work disturbances, marital conflict, and financial problems. This was the path Tommy's parents were on. Although they had good intentions for Tommy, they lost sight of how and where to direct their energy. Tommy's mom loved him so much and wanted nothing more than to see him succeed in school and life. Unfortunately, it seemed like the harder she tried, the worse it got, and both she and her husband felt like they were nagging him all the time. In Tommy's case, we were able to intervene before the family experienced serious consequences. I was touched by the courage Tommy's parents exhibited in stepping forward and facing their issues head-on, and I praised them for their hard work.

If you have a child who has been struggling and doesn't seem like their old self, you are not alone. We are all aware of the turbulence of being a teenager. That said, some unique circumstances in today's world have contributed to many children struggling socially and emotionally and being unprepared to take on the rigors of school and life. We have all been hearing about this new "internet generation" of kids born after 1995, who have grown up alongside the advent of the internet, cell phones, and other wireless devices.

Dr. Jean Twenge, a researcher and psychology professor at San Diego State University, has studied generational differences for twenty-five years and coined the term "iGen," meaning "internet generation." iGen kids are the first to experience their entire adolescence on cell phones. Consequently, Dr. Twenge reports that kids have become more isolated from each other, resulting in serious social and emotional deficits necessary to develop through adolescence and adulthood. These deficits have been further exacerbated by the advent of COVID-19 and are consistent with a historic increase in the mental health problems experienced by our children. Mental fitness struggles are presenting themselves in high schools and college campuses, with a spike in suicide and dropout rates that run parallel to the technology boom. I have developed a mental fitness process to address these deficits and get your child on track for success. Let's review a widely accepted framework that illustrates how our children, under normal conditions, develop these very important social and emotional skills.

Abraham Maslow talks about the process of self-actualization as a theory of motivation. Self-actualization is something we all strive for as human beings, and parents want this for their children. To reach a level in life where we are doing what we were born to do, we have needs that have to be met along the way. Maslow presents it as a pyramid. We start at the bottom (1) and reach for the top (5).

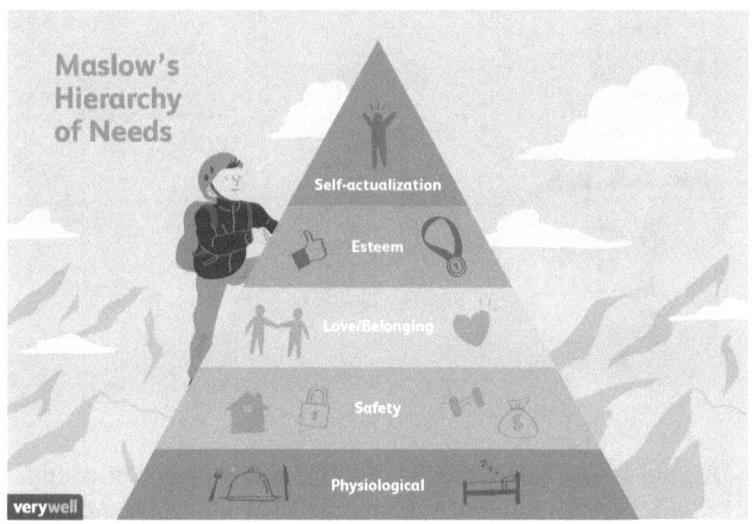

1. Physiological: food, water, shelter, warmth, and sleep.
2. Safety: the need to feel secure, stable, and unafraid.
3. Love and belonging: the need to belong socially by developing relationships with friends and family.
4. Esteem: the need to feel self-esteem based on one's achievements and abilities and recognition and respect from others.

5. Self-actualization: the need to pursue and fulfill one's unique potential.

My mental fitness hierarchy shares similarities with Maslow's pyramid. We start at the bottom, making sure we have your child's basic needs in place and attending to foundational skills. Foundational skills correspond with Maslow's physiological and safety needs. They are the basic and very important skills your child needs to navigate through life, such as managing time and money, getting good sleep, minding nutrition, and incorporating sufficient physical activity into daily routines.

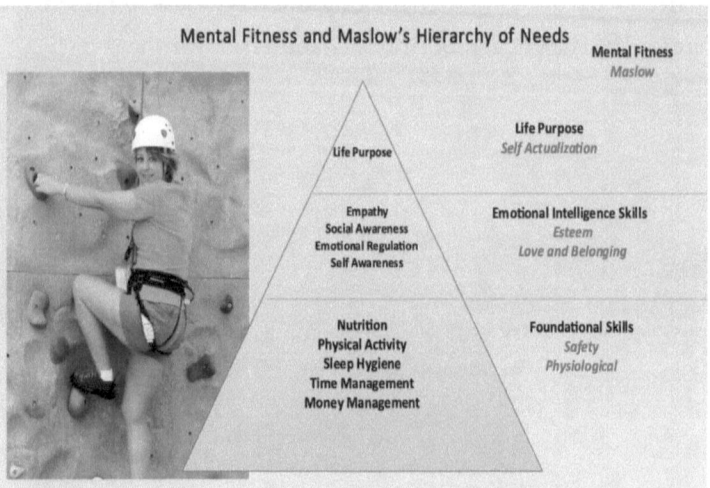

A solid foundation lends itself to the development of confidence and healthy self-esteem. The second phase of my process focuses on developing social and emotional skills, commonly called "emotional intelligence skills." These skills correspond with Maslow's love, belongingness, and esteem needs. Examples of emotional intelligence skills are self-awareness, self-management, social skills, and empathy. Developing these skills enables your child to become aware that they are part of something larger than themselves and puts them on the path to discovering their life purpose. This corresponds with the final step in Maslow's hierarchy, self-actualization—reaching one's full potential.

Tommy's mom makes a good argument. Time is running out. The teenage years go by very quickly. It may not seem that way when we are in the trenches with our kids, feeling overwhelmed and tired. Don't worry. I am here to help you. I am also extremely excited to share this transformational process with you. In these next few years, you have an opportunity to rally and connect with your child like never before. If you were running a marathon, a couple miles from the finish line, and I were your coach, I would be encouraging and cheering you on. "Keep going! I know it's tiring! Don't give up. You're almost there! You've got this! It will be totally worth it! You'll be so happy that you stuck with it!" This is a defining moment in your marathon. I'm here with you. Let's do this!

CHAPTER 2:

Riding the Big Red with A Sour Taste in My Mouth

I COME FROM a very large Irish Catholic family. Growing up as a baby boomer, life was different than it is now. For example, we played outside all the time, neighborhoods were like an extension of the family, and we were in each other's yards and houses every day. The families were also much larger, and kids were everywhere! As a psychologist and coach, perhaps that's how I ended up in a profession that allows me to be around kids and families every day.

My mother was in her early twenties when she married my father, and by her early thirties, she had given birth to ten children. Imagine nine kids running around a three-bedroom house, with two sets of triple bunk beds and always a crib or two with a baby. I had a twin brother who passed away a few days after we were born. We were both very small, and medical care for preemies wasn't nearly as advanced as it is today. I was a very active child, sometimes a bit too active. Unbeknownst to our family at the time, I later learned that I had attention deficit hyperactivity disorder (ADHD) and a nonverbal learning disability, which manifests in significant visual-spatial deficits. Following an assessment I had as an adult, I was told, "David, an engineer you'll never be."

Although my family was low in monetary resources, we were rich in spirit. As much as we struggled financially, my parents instilled values of service in us. For that, I am eternally grateful. I would not trade my life experience for anything, for our experiences shape who we become and what we put out in the world. I will say that I have spent many years making mistakes and learning the hard way as I have strived to get to the top of my pyramid.

When I hit my teen years, I had some struggles. I was disorganized, angry, impulsive, and living life with a chip on my shoulder. I also went through a phase of running away from home quite frequently. One night, after coming home drunk, angry, and threatening to run away again, my parents called the police. Ultimately, I ended up in a juvenile detention center. From there, I was moved to a shelter, followed by a treatment center for several months. Initially, I was defensive and resistant to receiving help and being honest with myself. As time went on, I began to develop trusting relationships with the adults in charge of my care. I responded to their positive feedback and the lessons they taught. I began to feel a more solid foundation under me. I was only fifteen years old, and by the grace of God, I made it back home and graduated from high school.

I made my first attempt at college when I was nineteen years old. It was far more rigorous than high school, and my foundation began to crumble. I got mostly Fs my first semester and dropped out. I continued to enroll and drop out for the next several years, and my self-esteem was in the toilet. My sole sources of esteem and pleasure included running marathons and working out.

Working as a waiter in a busy restaurant in Minneapolis, a few miles from the University of Minnesota, I met a local fitness celebrity who encouraged me to compete in a seven-week fitness contest at a popular nightclub. I gave it my all, and I won. I was in orbit! Finally, I had achieved something to be proud of. My girlfriend, who I was crazy in love with, shattered my world when I gave her the news. I thought she would be thrilled with my victory. However, to my chagrin, she said, "That's great, but if you don't get a college education, I don't think it's going to work out with us." I was crushed. I will never forget sitting on that city bus, the "Big Red," off to the University of Minnesota, with a sour taste in my mouth, making yet another

Problem Discussion #3: Substance Use

Jack's mom asked me, "Do you think my son is an alcoholic?" Upon hearing this, I spoke with her about the difference between abuse and dependency. A lot of teens binge drink and get intoxicated. When substance use becomes so serious and prevalent that it impairs someone's ability to function in major life areas, such as work, school, relationships, or maintaining health, we start looking at it as a dependency. Dealing with substance use with teens is tricky. Most teens who go through chemical dependency treatment do not remain abstinent for the rest of their lives. If they are in danger with substance use and self-destructive, chemical dependency treatment can provide safety and education moving forward.

Diversion is another way to look at coping with addictive behaviors in kids. The more socially engaged kids are in school, sports, hobbies, and things they like to do, the easier it is to stay away from harmful substances. It is no fun to have something you like taken away, especially when you are struggling emotionally and if it makes you feel better. If something more important and exciting is added, it can naturally push the substance away without feeling like it was taken away from you against your will. Jack's alcohol use was risky and dangerous. And the fact that his father struggled with alcohol was an additional risk factor. Substance use and mental health struggles can pass through generations. I coached Jack's mom to think about working with him around chemical use as an ongoing process, where she would assist him in learning from consequences and developing strategies to be safe. I continued to assess Jack's chemical use and related consequences as our work progressed. He was able to learn from his mistakes and utilize diversionary activities to curb his substance use. I coached his parents to facilitate a meeting between Jack and his hockey coach. Eventually, Jack returned to the hockey team and committed himself to abstinence from alcohol and drugs during the season.

If you are worried that your child or anyone else in your family has a substance abuse problem, you can access a twenty-four seven, 365-day-a-year national helpline through the Substance Abuse and Mental Health Services Administration:

SAMHSA @ https://www.samhsa.gov/find-help/national-helpline

Problem Discussion #4: Mental Health

In addition to wondering if he was an alcoholic, Jack's mom wanted to know if he had depression. It is normal for your child to experience depression or anxiety in their teen years. As in our discussion about chemical use, if it gets to a point where it seriously jeopardizes your child's ability to function in school, in a job, or in relationships, or causes serious physical health threats, getting professional help is a good idea. I assessed Jack for depression and anxiety. While experiencing symptoms of both, he didn't fit the full criteria for either diagnosis. Instead, Jack's condition more accurately fit the diagnostic criteria for adjustment disorder, with mixed disturbance of emotions and conduct. In other words, Jack was reacting to situational stressors, such as his parents' divorce and the pressures of high school. My prescription for Jack was to participate in individual and family therapy without medication. Had Jack's symptoms persisted or worsened during therapy, I would have referred him for a medication assessment.

Summary

Were you able to identify with any parts of this story? Although Jack's case was extreme and covered many important problem areas experienced by teens, it was by no means a comprehensive study. Your child may have some struggles that Jack didn't. If you want to help your child overcome hurdles to mental fitness and success, you will need to learn about sources of stress. To learn about the sources of stress your teen is experiencing and how they are coping, it is very important to have honest and open conversations with them.

Chapter 4 Assignment #1:

Below is a list of common triggers of teen stress. Use this list as an assessment tool by discussing each of these stressors with your child. Have your child rate each area on a scale of zero to ten, where zero is no stress at all and ten is the highest possible stress they could experience. Record the numerical ratings your child gives you in your journal. You and your child can take this assessment again at the end of this process to measure your progress.

- **Academic Stress**

From grades to test scores to applying to college, teens experience high levels of school-related stress. Many teens worry about meeting academic demands, pleasing teachers and parents, and keeping up with their classmates. Poor time management skills can also play into academic stress.

- **Social Stress**

Teens place a high value on their social lives and spend most of their waking hours among peers. Finding and keeping friend groups can be stressful. Bullying and subtle instances of relational aggression are clear sources of stress. Learning to manage conflict and work through romantic relationships are also significant sources of stress for developing teens. Peer pressure is an additional source of anxiety. To establish and maintain friendships, teens can engage in behavior outside of their comfort zones to appease their peers.

- **Family Problems**

Unrealistic expectations, marital problems, strained sibling relationships (including sibling bullying), illness, and financial stress can all trigger a spike in teen stress.

- **World Events**

School shootings, acts of terrorism, and natural disasters worry parents but also trigger stress for teens. Teens are often privy to the twenty-four-hour news cycle, and hearing bits and pieces of scary news, both domestic and abroad, can leave teens wondering about their safety and the safety of their loved ones.

- **Traumatic Events**

Death of a family member or friend, accidents, sickness, or enduring emotional or physical abuse can impact teen stress levels. It's also important to note that approximately 10 percent of teens are impacted by dating violence in the form of verbal, physical, or sexual abuse.

- **Significant Life Changes**

Like adults, teens experience stress due to significant life changes. Moving, starting at a new school, and changes in the makeup of the family, including divorce and blended families, can trigger stress for teens. Not knowing how to cope with big changes is overwhelming and can confuse your child.

Chapter 4 Assignment #2:

When you finish this assessment, continue writing in your journal about the following: What are your concerns for your child? What are your hopes and dreams?

CHAPTER 5:

Step 2—What's Happening in Your World?

What's Your Style?

BASED ON OUR childhood experiences, we develop parenting styles. Much has been written in research about parenting styles, and many categories have been designated. To keep things simple, I am going to share three styles from developmental psychologist Dr. Diana Baumrind. These are the most common ones I run into in my practice. As you learn about them, think about how they relate to how you were parented and how they impact your current parenting style. What I don't want you to do is cement yourself into any one of these categories. Remember, we are not perfect. Sometimes we are on a roll as parents, doing a good job, and sometimes we struggle and make mistakes. This is about becoming self-aware so we can be more effective in helping our kids succeed in school and life.

- **Authoritarian/Strict and Controlling:** This style has been linked to the most unfortunate consequences for healthy child development. It is characterized by parents having a high need for behavioral control and a strict family hierarchy. Parents implement strict rules and leave no room for discussion with their kids. They encourage the suppression of emotions, and they can also become aggressive and angry. Rules are typically enforced via threats and punishment. Kids of authoritarian parents quickly learn to adjust to their parent's expectations. In other words, they are well-behaved out of fear. "If I don't behave, I will be punished!" They tend to obey authorities willingly. They have an internalized and accepted prevailing norm and value system, which means they do relatively well in school and do not engage in deviant behavior, such as criminal acts or experimental drug or alcohol use. They are not used to making independent choices or taking full responsibility for themselves. They do not experiment much with new ways of doing things or alternative ways of thinking. According to research, kids from authoritarian parents are less socially skilled than authoritative and permissive parents. They find it difficult to handle frustration; girls give up in the face of challenges, and boys react aggressively. They are also more prone to low self-esteem, anxiety, and depression.

- **Permissive:** Permissive parents are at the other end of the spectrum. They believe in individual autonomy and see the world as a free place, filled with opportunities just waiting to be seized. Permissive parents believe in responding to their children's desires in an accepting and empathetic manner. The child is viewed as a child and is not expected to behave according to mature or adult standards. Traditional child discipline and rigid rules of conduct are seen as restrictive to a child's natural development and free, independent thinking. Children are perceived as equals, included in decision-making processes, and encouraged to communicate and discuss rather than just obey. Permissive parents dislike and tend to avoid confrontations and the overt use of power to shape and regulate their child's behavior. These kids are brought up believing they are adult equals, well equipped in dialogue, and have high social skills, high self-esteem, and low levels of depression. On the flip side, kids who lack limits, have an absence of authority figures, and have no consistent routines or predictability may experience a sense of insecurity. "How far can I go, and what can I count on?" In response to a parent who avoids conflict, the child may become bossy or dominating as they try to search for limits where there are none. Because of the instilled beliefs that the world is open for experimentation and there are very few musts, children of permissive parents are found to be more impulsive and involved in problematic behavior, such as drug and alcohol use, and do less well in school than kids from authoritative and authoritarian parents.

- **Authoritative:** Most parenting experts agree that this is the most constructive style. Like authoritarian parents, the authoritative parent's control is firm, and the standards of behavior are high. The difference is that authoritative parents do not keep their children down or restrict them as a preventative measure for bad behavior. The authoritative parents strive toward letting their children live out their potential but within an overall controlled framework. "You can go as far as this point, but exceeding this boundary will not be tolerated." In this way, the authoritative parents recognize that a child needs to have a degree of say but will always make sure to have the final word. They strive to balance a child's need for autonomy and their own need for discipline and control. Authoritative parents use praise and positive attention to make their child want to behave well. "If I behave and do well, I will get positive attention." Authoritative parents try to understand their children and teach them how to understand their own feelings. They encourage problem-solving and independence. Because of positive reinforcement (praise) along with logical and fair rules, done in a warm, caring manner, the child has learned that behaving and following rules feels good and gets them positive attention. Their ability to decode and live up to their parent's rules and expectations provides them with well-developed social skills and emotional regulation. According to research, kids of authoritative parents do well in school, are self-confident, and are goal oriented.

What's Your Story?

We all grow up with a unique set of circumstances that become our story, and our story has an impact on how we parent our children. Being an effective parent isn't as much about whether you had a good or bad childhood. It's more about looking back and connecting the dots. It's about recognizing how your childhood experience gets replayed in your mind as you engage with your teen. You might think, *Oh. okay. This is the same thing I experienced when I was that age. That's why I get triggered when my daughter talks back.* Or *Oh, I see, my mom used to get terrified when I didn't come home on time and would yell and scream at me. That's why I get so scared when my child doesn't come home on time.*

When we can understand how we get from point A to point B (connecting the dots), we can step back and check ourselves without feeling like we are failures as parents. When we get frustrated and yell at our kids, most of the time, it's about us, not them. As a parent, I try not to yell at my kids and have been mostly successful but have not always been perfect. Have you ever yelled at your child, and suddenly, your mom or dad pops into your head? You think to yourself, *I can't believe it. I'm doing exactly what I said I would never do.* If you aren't aware of where you have been, you are more likely to be reactive versus proactive. It's like automatic pilot versus mindful parenting.

Richard's Story

This is a story with an unhappy ending. An old client, a friend of Richard's, referred him to me for parent coaching. Richard was in his mid-forties and the father of two adolescent boys. Prior to coming to see me, Richard had been experiencing a great deal of conflict with his younger son. I engaged Richard in several discussions, exploring his family of origin and how he was parented as a child. Richard described his parents as old-school. His mother worked part-time at the neighborhood grocery store but mostly stayed home to take care of the family. His father was a hardworking man who owned a small construction company and drank heavily on the weekends. Richard spoke lovingly of his parents, but it was clear that he was raised in an authoritarian environment, where physical punishment was administered frequently. At one point in our discussions, Richard said of his father, "Man, he could hit hard and yell like nobody's business!" Richard described his mother as sweet and loving. He would go to her for comfort after receiving physical punishment from his dad. When his father wasn't around, Richard's mom treated him like an adult and allowed him to do whatever he wanted.

As our work progressed, Richard shared stories about his relationship with his children as they grew from infancy to adolescence. As little kids, if they misbehaved, he would give them a swat on their behind, a slap on the hand, or yell at them sternly. He felt like he was doing the right thing because they would comply. When they reached adolescence, the power struggles escalated, and his attempts at controlling his children's behavior became more severe. Yelling turned into screaming, and swats turned into more physical forms of punishment. His older child would usually get in line, but his younger child began to rebel. The more defiant and oppositional his son was, the more extreme Richard's disciplinary tactics became. At his core, Richard loved his children deeply and would feel remorseful after punishing them harshly. To make it up to them, he would give them gifts, be permissive, and overlook many of the household rules that he and his wife had agreed upon.

In my efforts to get Richard to connect the dots, I had him examine his parenting methods and compare them to how he was raised. His harsh disciplinary practices mirrored his father's style, while his attempts to make up for it reflected his mother's style. This was very confusing not only for his son but for the rest of the family. Although Richard was able to talk about how his father had strict control of his family and how he was mistreated, he was unable to see how he had recreated the same dynamic in his family and was unwilling to make the necessary changes. Unfortunately, his youngest son, who was struggling in school and the community, eventually left home. They continue to be estranged from one another.

My Story

I went through a turbulent period with my son as he was entering early adolescence. He was doing what teens do—testing limits and taking some risks—but nothing out of the norm for teen behavior. His behavior was triggering me, and I would get mad and yell at him. As a mental health professional and coach, a little voice told me that yelling was not helpful. I struggled for a few months to keep my composure with him. We finally had a chat one day. He told me that he felt demoralized when I yelled at him. The yelling made him want to rebel rather than comply. Intuitively, I knew this to be true, yet it was difficult for me to check myself in the heat of the moment. When I reflected on my experiences growing up, it became clear that, like Richard's father, my father leaned more toward the authoritarian style. There were so many of us to take care of, and he felt he needed to be strict to keep us safe and under control. I was a very active child (remember, undiagnosed ADHD), and some of my impulsive behaviors got me into trouble. Looking back at it, I probably scared my dad half to death! While he never used physical punishment, I was yelled at and frequently grounded for long periods of time.

In my own experience of connecting the dots, I realized that my son's entry into adolescence triggered me. Ages fourteen and fifteen were the rockiest period in my teen years, and my son's behavior was pushing my buttons. My yelling was more about me than his behavior. I was unconsciously recreating my family dynamic. After some practice and deep breathing, I began to yell less. It greatly improved our communication.

As parents, we don't need to condemn ourselves for making mistakes and yelling at our children. Most of us have been there. We don't have to be right all the time with our kids. We can apologize and mend fences. And while yelling may stop a behavior in the moment, it doesn't teach our kids the behaviors we are looking for. It is impossible to communicate and express love through harsh discipline. Our children are more willing to listen to us and accept limits if they feel loved and understood.

Chapter 5 Assignment:

Connect the Dots: In your journal, answer the following questions. How has your childhood experience benefited your parenting style? Which childhood experiences do you need to be aware of that may result in making mistakes? What example do you want to set for your kids? What values do you want to pass on to them?

CHAPTER 6:

Step 3—Understanding Your iGen's Unique World

ACCORDING TO THE Center for Generational Kinetics, "a generation is a group of people *born* around the same time and *raised* around the same place. People in this 'birth cohort' exhibit similar characteristics, preferences, and values over their lifetimes." For example, I am a baby boomer. We are individuals born between 1946 and 1964, who grew up with the Beatles, the Vietnam War, Woodstock, and the Apollo moon landings. We were profoundly impacted by television. The generation following me is Generation X, born between 1961 and 1980. Generation X witnessed the end of the Cold War, the fall of the Berlin Wall, Live Aid, and the personal computer. Next up is Generation Y, more commonly referred to as millennials. These folks were born between 1981 and 1996. Their formative experiences were the 9/11 terrorist attacks, the Sony PlayStation, social media, and reality TV.

This chapter focuses on the current generation and its unique influences and challenges. Common characteristics of iGeners are:

- Much more tolerant of others (e.g., different cultures, sexual orientations, and races)
- Much more cautious and less risk-taking
- Less drinking and drug consumption in high school
- Less likely to go to church

- More likely to think for themselves and not believe authority figures in the church or government
- Delaying having serious romantic relationships
- Less teen pregnancy
- Fewer runaways
- Delaying driving and fewer teen driving accidents
- Less time spent in shopping malls
- Less likely to go out to see a movie
- More likely to use Instagram than Facebook
- Less in-person and face to face contact with others due to more time connecting via smartphones
- Heavy use of gaming
- Less reading of books and newspapers
- Grew up more supervised and more protected than prior generations
- Less experience with teen jobs and earning money in high school
- May stay up until 2 a.m. using their smartphone and social media

Challenge Discussion #1: Teen Brain

As you coach your child to become more mentally fit, it is important to have some basic information about brain biology. We know that the brain doesn't fully develop until age twenty-five. Below is a visual aid to help you understand how your child's brain develops.

Much like our earlier discussion of Maslow's pyramid, the brain develops from the bottom up. Researchers have referred to the bottom or lower brain as the reptilian brain. This is because reptiles were among the first life-forms on the planet. Think about a lizard sitting on a rock sunning itself. Not the cute Geico lizard you see in commercials who has been infused with human qualities, but an actual lizard. It simply sits in the sun. It's not concerned about what it will wear to school tomorrow. It doesn't feel sad because its best friend ghosted it on Instagram. Its only concern is survival: eating, breathing, keeping warm, and reproducing. As infants, this is the primary part of the brain we function from.

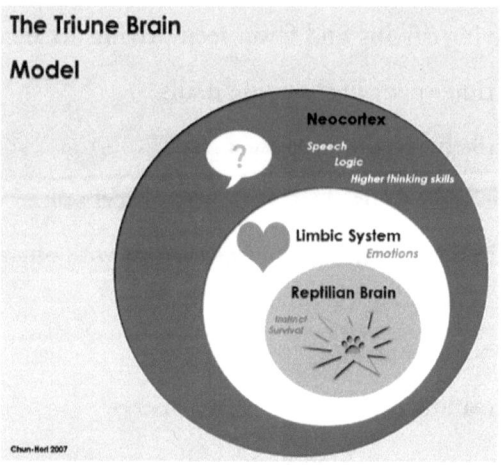

As our children mature into the preteen and teen years, brain development occurs in the limbic system. The limbic system is the emotional part of the brain. This part feels emotions, empathy, the need for social connection, and a sense of values. This is also the part of the brain where people can get stuck. It's like a Neanderthal, with very raw emotions. And while they need social affiliation, they are not skilled enough to express emotions appropriately. Think of an adolescent boy attempting to show a girl that he likes her by roughly patting her on the back or bringing her a dead frog as a gift.

The neocortex, the outer part of the brain, is the most sophisticated and highly developed. This part of the brain utilizes logic, searches for meaning, and makes rational decisions. This is where we want to be as we mature into adulthood.

Neuropsychiatrist Dr. Dan Siegal refers to the adolescent brain as a "brain under construction." Development starts from the base of the brain, moving up toward the front from lower- to higher-level functions. The end goal is the development of an "integrated brain." Emotions are mediated by rational thought for the sake of our children's ability to control impulses and make sound decisions. Teens with lesser developed thinking and planning parts of their brains have a much quicker route to their emotional center, resulting in what has been referred to by researchers and clinicians as "limbic lava." Teenagers are predisposed to volcanic eruptions of raw emotion that can get quite hot. It is the job of the brain's higher thinking and planning part (neocortex) to cool the limbic lava. When our children cannot cope with raw emotions and think rationally, they need guidance and support to make good decisions.

I vividly remember the day my sixteen-year-old daughter came home from her driver's license test. She had not only just passed but also done it on her first attempt. She was in orbit! I stopped her in mid-sprint as she grabbed my car keys from the kitchen table. We were both simultaneously incensed. I was frustrated because she didn't ask if she could take the car, and she couldn't believe I was questioning her. After all, she had just passed her test. What could possibly go wrong now? Sparks were flying, to say the least! Brain-based researchers would agree that, in that moment, my daughter and I were having a failure to communicate from a biological perspective. It is well established that the brain's emotional center in the limbic system matures earlier than the higher-order thinking and planning part of the brain (neocortex). Activated limbic lava made it very difficult for my daughter to focus and answer the "who, what, when, where, and why" of my questions. "How can you not let me go? I just passed my test! Please, just let me go!" I assisted her by taking a breath, slowing myself down, and providing an explanation for my questions. When she became convinced that it was about her safety, she participated in planning.

Knowledge of limbic lava does not allow us to ignore our teen's eruptions, nor for them to erupt whenever they want. If we view these eruptions as events that must be corrected immediately, however, we could inadvertently be setting ourselves and our children up for failure. If we view our teenager's development not as an event but as an ongoing process, we will have better success. An adolescent's path to a fully developed thinking and planning neocortex can take ten to fifteen years and extend into the mid-twenties.

Challenge Discussion #2: COVID-19 and Your Child

As you may already know and will learn more about in the next section, before the pandemic, children's mental health was as poor as ever and consistent with the rise of wireless technology, cell phones, and social media. Two years into the pandemic, we experienced greater mental health fallout. According to a special report on children's mental health and COVID-19, from the American Psychological Association, "Mental illness and the demand for psychological services are at an all-time high—especially among children." Within the first year of the pandemic, mental health-related emergency room visits went up by 24 percent for children ages five to eleven and 31 percent for ages twelve to seventeen. Access to timely mental health services was a problem before and now even more post-COVID. There simply aren't enough trained mental health professionals in schools or outpatient clinics to meet the demand. As a result, mental health professionals are focusing on preventative approaches by sharing knowledge and training with teachers and school staff about social and emotional skills (emotional intelligence) to help kids cope with stress. In the same way, I am equipping you, parents, with the same knowledge in my mental fitness framework that is preventative and will help your child thrive through adolescence and early adulthood.

Challenge Discussion #3: Cell Phones and Social Media

In her book, Dr. Twenge identifies eleven major trends with our iGen kids. One of the most alarming negative trends is a dramatic decline in social and emotional skills. Through her research, Dr. Twenge estimated that our kids are three years behind socially and emotionally. Imagine your fifteen-year-old on a college campus or attempting to live independently for the first time. There is strong evidence that cell phones and other forms of wireless technology are the culprits. Kids are spending more time with their cell phones than with each other. Take a look at these trends:

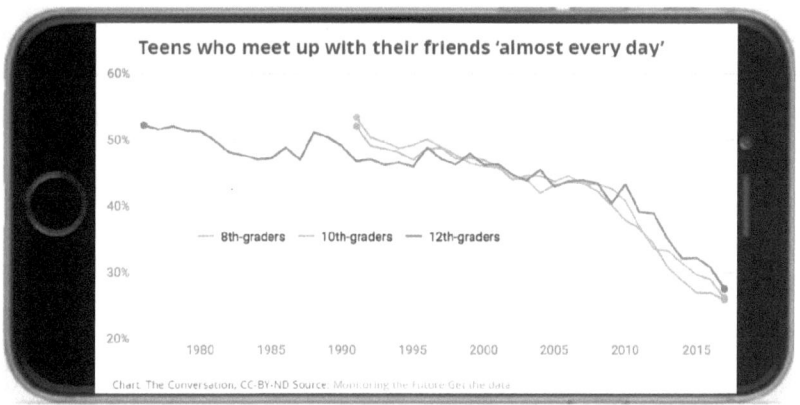

The numbers on the left represent the percentage of teens who spend time with their friends almost daily. The numbers on the bottom represent the years beginning from 1980 to 2015. Since the mid-1990s, there has been a dramatic decrease in the percentage of kids who spend time with each other almost daily. In the early- to mid-1990s, approximately 54 percent of teens met up with their friends regularly. By 2015, the percentage of teens meeting regularly dropped by nearly 30 percent. And look at the reverse trend below.

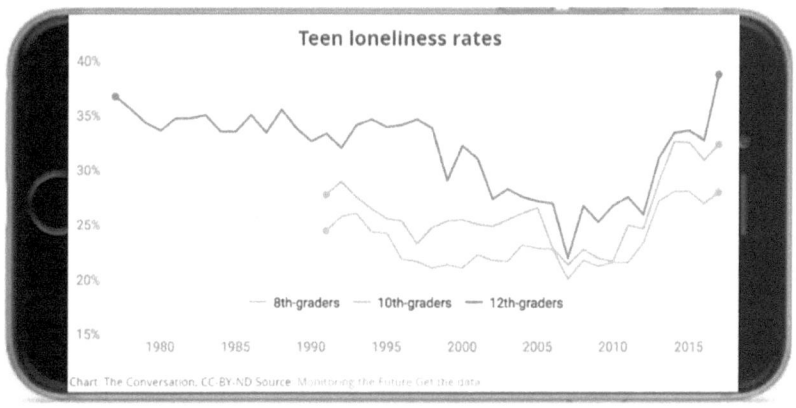

Teen loneliness rates have skyrocketed! Take note of the spike from 2010 to 2015. According to the Pew Research Center, smartphone ownership crossed the 50 percent threshold in late 2012, right when teen depression and suicide began to rise. By 2015, 73 percent of teens had access to smartphones. And as teen loneliness has gone up, so has the prevalence of mental health disorders. In a survey by Dr. Keith Anderson, president of the American College Health Association Survey, one in three college freshmen reported having suffered from mental health disorders before coming to college.

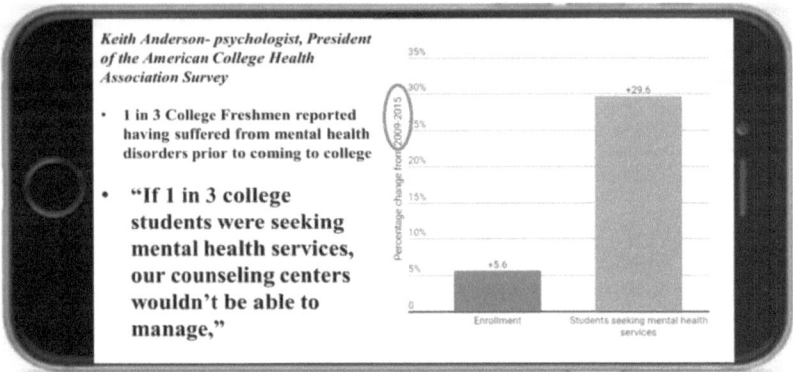

From 2009 to 2015, college students seeking mental health services increased by 29.6 percent. Colleges are not even close to being able to handle this demand. There appears to be a correlation between the increase in mental health issues and suicide rates, as illustrated by the diagram below.

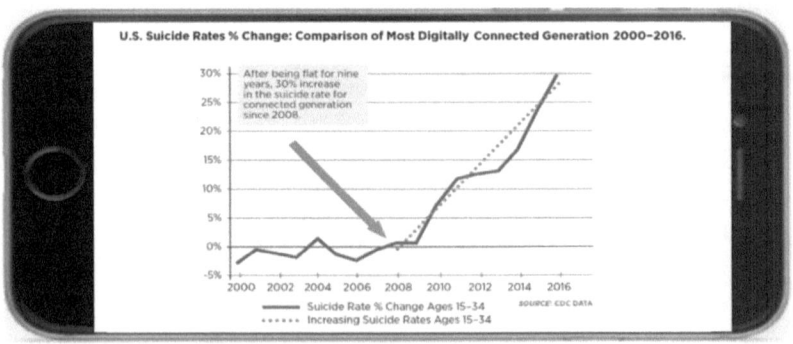

As you can see, suicide rates were relatively flat from 1999 to 2008. From 2009 to 2016, the suicide rate for teens and young adults went up 30 percent, almost exactly the same as the ratio of college students seeking mental health services in this time period, 29.6 percent.

My intent here is not to tell you that cell phones and wireless technology have definitively caused this spike in mental health struggles, school problems, and suicides. To come to such a conclusion, you must conduct scientific studies and have them evaluated by the research community. That said, these are trends we cannot ignore. When I look at the data, I see an alarming series of trends that appear to be the formula for a perfect storm:

- Increased screen time leads to less face-to-face contact.
- Less face-to-face contact leads to increased loneliness.
- Increased loneliness leads to a decrease in social and emotional skills.
- A decrease in social and emotional skills leads to increased mental health disorders and problems at home, schools, and college campuses.
- Increases in mental health disorders lead to an increase in suicide rates.

In 1995, at the onset of the internet generation, Dr. Dan Goleman, a modern-day guru on social and emotional skills, wrote the book, *Emotional Intelligence: Why It Can Matter More Than IQ*. Here is a quote from his book: "Will these tech-savvy children become adults who are as comfortable with other people as they are with their computers? I suspected that a childhood relating to the virtual world would deskill our young people when it comes to relating to people." It appears as if his suspicions were right on the money!

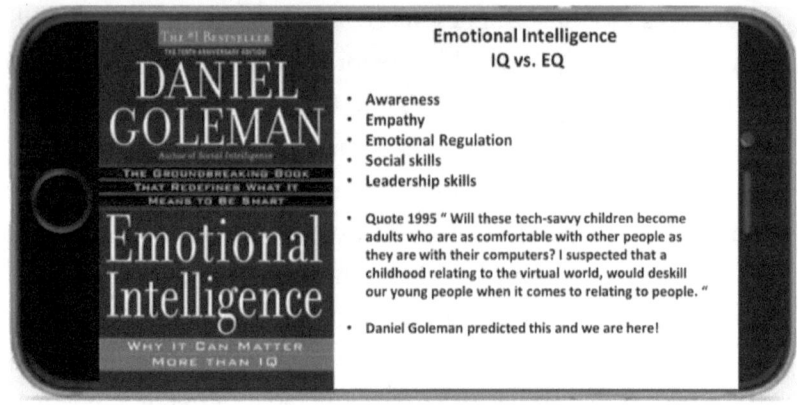

This is a topic that is being heavily researched, and we will be getting more information moving forward. Dr. Twenge, in her research, has noted that problems begin to occur when screen time exceeds two hours per day. How much screen time is your child engaging in each day? How much screen time are you engaging in each day?

Parents, there are several apps out there that monitor your children's screen habits and keep them safe. *Net Nanny* is an example of parental control software that allows you to track your family's digital activities in real time and make informed decisions about screen time. Internet filters block harmful content, and instant alerts notify you if your child is searching for topics such as pornography, drugs, suicide, or weapons. You can increase or decrease the daily allocation of screen time and turn off the internet if you choose.

Secure Teen is an app that allows you to review call logs and read text messages. *Teen Safe* is a similar app that allows parents to monitor call logs, read text messages, track exact "GPS" locations, and freeze their child's phone so they can't text while driving. While these are potentially very useful apps, you are best off being honest and upfront with your kids about which ones you are using and why. You also need to consider their age and maturity levels when making decisions about privacy, which may require some negotiation. Below are some links you can access to get more information on internet safety and social media use.

https://internetsafety101.org/parentsguidetosocialmedia

http://www.princetoncommonground.org/wp-content/uploads/2017/03/parents-guide-to-social-media.pdf

https://www.youngminds.org.uk/parent/parents-a-z-mental-health-guide/social-media/

Challenge Discussion #4: Depression and Anxiety

In chapter three, I discussed the sharp increase in anxiety and depression experienced among our iGen kids. In my practice, when a client exhibits symptoms of depression or anxiety, I make an assessment to determine the root cause. In some cases, the cause appears to be a biological or neurological issue that requires medication. In other cases, the root cause may be situational or environmental, requiring therapy or coaching. Occasionally, the client needs both. From my perspective, the root cause of the increase in mental health problems that our iGen kids experience is environmental.

Depression and anxiety affect teens regardless of gender, social background, income level, or other achievements. Common risk factors are:

- Family history of depression and anxiety—between 20 to 50 percent of teens with depression or anxiety have a family member who suffers from depression/anxiety or another mental health disorder
- Experiencing trauma, abuse, or long-term illness or disability
- Being bullied
- Excessive screen time
- Previous episodes of depression/anxiety
- LGBTQIA children who get harassed by other kids for sexual orientation or gender identity
- When a friend commits suicide
- Addiction to drugs or alcohol

Signs and symptoms of depression are as follows:

- Persistent feelings of sadness, irritability, or tension
- Loss of interest in usual activities or hobbies
- A change in appetite, with a significant weight loss or gain
- A change in sleeping patterns, such as difficulty sleeping, early morning awakening, or sleeping too much
- Restlessness or feeling slowed down
- Decreased ability to make decisions or concentrate
- Feelings of worthlessness, hopelessness, or guilt
- Thoughts of suicide or death

Signs and symptoms of anxiety are as follows:

- Excessive worry occurring more days than not for at least six months
- Difficulty controlling worries
- Restlessness or feeling keyed up or on edge
- Being easily fatigued
- Difficulty concentrating or mind going blank
- Irritability
- Muscle Tension
- Sleep disturbance

As a least restrictive measure, you can work with your child on the mental fitness approach I offer in this book. However, if you believe your child is experiencing more serious depression or anxiety, you have options. You can start by talking with your pediatrician. They can refer you to psychiatric resources, such as medication, or psychological resources, such as therapy, coaching, or mentoring.

Challenge Discussion # 5: Bullying

In an article from *Psychology Today*, bullying is described as "a distinctive pattern of harming and humiliating others; specifically, those who are in some way smaller, weaker, younger, or in any way more vulnerable than the bully. Bullying is not garden-variety aggression; it is a deliberate and repeated attempt to cause harm to others of lesser power. It's a very durable behavioral style, largely because bullies get what they want, at least at first. Bullies are made, not born, and it happens at an early age if the normal aggression of 2-year-olds isn't handled with consistency. Between 1 in 4 and 1 in 3 students in the United States report being bullied at school, according to the National Center for Education Statistics and Bureau of Justice Statistics. In grades 6 through 12 alone, over a quarter of students have experienced bullying. Electronic bullying has become a significant problem in the past decade. The ubiquity of hand-held devices affords bullies constant access to their prey, and harassment can often be carried out anonymously."

Bullying on social media is like bullying on steroids to a Gen-Xer or baby boomer. Periodic bullying in a parking lot behind the school, with fewer participants, is very different from the relentless bullying that can occur on social media, involving a much larger audience. A few years ago, I was tasked with responding to a shooting threat in a middle school. I conducted some groups with the kids to help them process the incident, and when we got to the bottom of it, we discovered that it was about bullying. I sat and listened to the kids in the group and was really concerned about their emotional health. Imagine trying to focus in a classroom under these conditions. I worked with these kids to change the group norm by empowering a couple of participants who were natural leaders. Some of the kids were aligned with the bully to be popular, and others were aligned with him out of fear. By being assertive with their thoughts and feelings, the leaders were able to inspire the rest of the group to abandon their allegiance with the bully. Talk about emotional intelligence! It was amazing to see these kids, many of whom didn't feel safe and secure under the care of adults at the school, stand up as a group to the bully in the classroom. Here are some tips for coaching your child to deal with bullying:

- Encourage your child to block bullies on cell phones and other forms of social media.
- Have them talk to a teacher or authority figure at school.
- Encourage your child to travel in pairs.
- Teach and encourage assertiveness skills.
- Regularly check in with your child to see if they have been subject to bullying.
- Consider enrolling your child in a social skills training group.

Challenge Discussion #6: Teen Suicide

I received a call a few years ago to provide psycho-educational support to a high school that experienced a teen suicide. Three months prior, as a parent of a high school teenager, my community experienced a tragic teen suicide. Most of us have been touched by teen suicide in one way or another, and we all grieve when children in our communities decide to take their life. Our children's sense of security can be threatened when they abruptly lose a close friend or acquaintance who commits suicide. School distress reaction often runs high, with so many kids fearful and grieving together. Administrators seeking my help reported a significant increase in student hospitalizations following the suicide in their school.

Suicide is the second leading cause of death for children and young adults between the ages of ten and twenty-four years old. There are an estimated twenty-five attempts for every completed suicide, and the risk increases dramatically when firearms are in the home. Overdose, using over-the-counter prescription and nonprescription medicine, is a common method for attempting and completing suicide. Teen girls think about and attempt suicide twice as often as boys. They tend to overdose on drugs and cut themselves, whereas teen boys die by suicide four times more often than girls. Boys are also prone to using more dangerous methods, such as firearms, hanging, and jumping from heights.

The impact following a suicide depends on how close our children were to the child who died or whether they were exposed to the trauma of witnessing distressing scenes. Feelings of guilt and anger are particularly pertinent to survivors. Kids may feel guilty for things they said or didn't say to their classmates who passed away. As parents, it is important to assure them that it was not their fault but rather a decision made by someone who was not well.

Parents, if you are struggling emotionally, it is important to get help for yourself so you are in a place to support your children. Talking to adults and keeping in touch with other parents is helpful. You may want to seek out counseling support if you are having a hard time helping your children. Here are some tips for supporting your teen:

- Expressing your feelings around them is okay if they are not out of control.
- Your child may need to talk to you a lot about the details of the incident itself.
- Keep the door open for them to share, and give them space if needed.
- If they witnessed the death or know someone who witnessed the death, this, in itself, is traumatic, and they may require professional help.
- Try to arrange an individual time to talk or just be together.
- Sometimes teenagers talk more to their friends than their parents. Your question as to how they are feeling may bring anger as a response. Understand that this is a common emotion expressed in grief.
- Make sure your teenagers know they are not responsible for the death.

- Encourage your teenager to go to the funeral or take part in any rituals to mark the life and death of the young person. Closure can be very healing.

To all affected by the loss of a child, friend, classmate, or community member, it is important to allow yourself time and ritual to grieve. As painful as it is to talk about or face when our community loses a child to suicide, we must support each other through our grief for the sake of healing. Here are some important points to know about grief:

- There are no right or wrong ways to experience grief.
- There is no secret method that will take grief away instantly.
- There are no rules to grief; everyone grieves differently.
- There is no timetable for grief.
- Grief becomes easier as time passes.
- Counseling may help you through the grief process.
- Take all the time and space you need to grieve your own way.

Challenge Discussion #7: Vaping Epidemic

The original intent of vaping products was to provide healthy alternatives to smoking by heating raw plant matter or extracts without combustion. For example, instead of burning substances such as marijuana or tobacco, vaping gently heats them to limit the release of harmful chemicals and maximize the plant's intended effects. In 2003, the first e-cigarette was approved in China. It made its way to the US in 2006. After 2006, the market for modern vaporizers grew tremendously. The first vaporizer for nicotine had the look and feel of a traditional cigarette. Since then, new manufacturers have created their own versions of liquids, chargers, and battery systems.

Unfortunately, the original intent of vaping as a healthy alternative to smoking has backfired and negatively impacted the health of our children. In December 2018, US Surgeon General Dr. Jerome Adams reported that teen vaping had reached epidemic levels, threatening to hook a new generation of people on nicotine. In a briefing, he disclosed, "We have never seen the use of any substance by America's young people rise this rapidly. This is an unprecedented challenge."

Following the results of a study in 2021, Mitch Zeller, director of the FDA's Center for Tobacco Products, reported being disturbed by the findings that 25 percent of teens use e-cigarettes and say they vape every day. In a news conference, Dr. Adams stated, "I am officially declaring e-cigarette use among youth an epidemic. Now is the time to act. We need to protect our young people from all tobacco products, including e-cigarettes." Seventy percent of teens report being exposed to e-cigarette advertising—marketing flavors such as mint, fruit, candy, and menthol. And many of them report not being aware they contain nicotine. The top three reasons teens start vaping are peer pressure, flavors, and stress relief. The most popular devices used by middle and high school kids are variations of the original e-cigarette and are commonly referred to as *mods*.

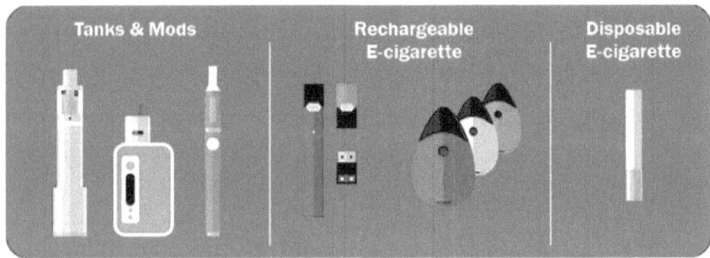

Parents, it is important to note these devices are dangerous because of the method of ingestion. They enable the user to take in very large amounts of nicotine that cross the blood-brain barrier extremely fast, resulting in nicotine toxicity. Some of these devices have been known to leak fluid, increasing the risk of being swallowed and poisoning the user. The Food and Drug Administration (FDA) reports budding evidence that these devices have been linked to cardiovascular problems and seizures, mostly among youth or young adult users. Here are some signs and symptoms that your child may be vaping:

- Unexplained sweet scents
- Pens or USB drivers that don't look normal
- Feeling queasy
- Vomiting
- Extreme thirst
- Smoker's cough
- Lung injury
- Diarrhea
- Seizures

Like smoking cigarettes, quitting vaping can be challenging, including withdrawal symptoms like cravings, headaches, irritability, and depression. The most common withdrawal symptoms from vaping are difficulty sleeping, excessive thirst, and concentration problems. Here are some tips for working with your child around vaping:

- **Start an open conversation.** Ideally, you want to have this conversation with your child before they are exposed to vaping. Ask them what they know about it. Be curious rather than punitive. "What have you heard about vaping? Do you know anyone who vapes?"

- **Educate yourself and your child.** If you explore this together, your child will be much less defensive and more responsive. There are hundreds of YouTube videos you can watch with your child. You may want to start by finding one that explains vaping in general and then move on to videos that educate on health risks and provide information on prevention.

- **Help your kids develop coping strategies and refusal skills.** As stated above, the top three reasons kids vape are due to peer pressure, flavors, and stress relief. Regarding peer pressure, the National Institute on Drug Abuse recommends, "Support teens to strategize ways to deflect the pressure to vape. For example, they might say simply, 'No, thanks,' or they could 'blame' it on you: 'My parents would kill me if I vaped!' They can also choose to spend some time with friends who don't vape." Kids like the flavors because they cover up the icky taste of nicotine, which, like with cigarettes, provides temporary stress relief. Nicotine, especially when vaped, activates dopaminergic systems in the brain that provide feelings of pleasure. The problem is, when dopamine is introduced unnaturally by nicotine or other substances, the brain will decrease its natural production, which results in anxiety and depression. This causes the user to need more and more of the substance to feel good and normal and is a recipe for addiction. As parents, we should educate and provide opportunities for our kids to activate their dopaminergic systems naturally. Below is a simple visual aid that identifies brain chemicals associated with feelings of well-being and strategies to boost their natural production.

SEROTONIN
THE HAPPY HORMONE

- LISTENING TO MUSIC
- MEDITATING
- WALK IN NATURE
- WRITING OR JOURNALING
- SUN EXPOSURE

DOPAMINE
THE REWARD CHEMICAL

- SELF-CARE
- COMPLETING TASKS
- EATING GOOD FOOD
- CELEBRATING WINS
- GETTING ENOUGH SLEEP

OXYTOCIN
THE LOVE DRUG

- HUGGING A LOVED ONE
- KISSING
- DEEP CONVERSATIONS
- PLAYING WITH ANIMALS
- GIVING COMPLIMENTS

ENDORPHIN
THE STRESS AND PAIN RELIEVER

- LAUGHING
- EXERCISE
- CHOCOLATE
- SPICY FOOD
- PHYSICAL TOUCH

- **Set a good example.** The best way to teach children anything is by example. In other words, don't vape; you know it's bad for you.

- **Set limits and enforce consequences.** Early on, it should be a rule of the house that children don't vape. Let them know their friends can't vape in the house either. Be clear about consequences and convey them in a way that's more about safety than punishment. Try your best to come up with fair and logical consequences, and make sure you follow through on them.

- **Make sure they get the help they need.** According to the National Institute on Drug Abuse, "If anxiety or depression is prompting your teen's vaping, they may need the support of a mental health professional to help them find healthy coping mechanisms. Moreover, if they have become addicted to nicotine or dependent on marijuana, they will need support to quit the vaping habit, along with therapy to address the underlying causes of substance abuse. Your family doctor is a good place to start the process."

Challenge discussion #8: Drug Dealers Targeting Teens Through Social Media Apps

I recently went on a golf outing with a friend whom I hadn't seen for quite a while. As we were getting caught up on family and work, he became emotional and spoke of an incident in which he received a phone call from his daughter that his son was in trouble. He suffered a drug overdose and needed help fast. He had been purchasing prescription drugs online for quite some time. The good news is that he recovered from his overdose, got proper treatment, and returned to a normal life. Also recently, I turned on the TV to watch the *Today* show. The hosts were interviewing the parents of a teen who had lost his life to a drug overdose. They shared back-and-forth messages through a social media app about a drug deal being made. The drugs were delivered right to the house. As my friend lamented when he told me his story, getting drugs is as easy as pushing a button on your phone.

The Organization of Social Media Safety reports drug dealing via social media is a serious, emerging social media-related threat. Research done prior to the pandemic indicates that about a quarter of teens have observed illegal drugs being advertised on social media. They are conducting new research and predict that this number has increased exponentially through the pandemic. In a period of about three minutes, your child can connect with a drug dealer and receive a menu of options. Teens that use social media regularly are five times as likely to smoke cigarettes, three times as likely to abuse alcohol, and twice as likely to use marijuana. Below is a menu of various drugs sent to a tester from the Organization of Social Media Safety.

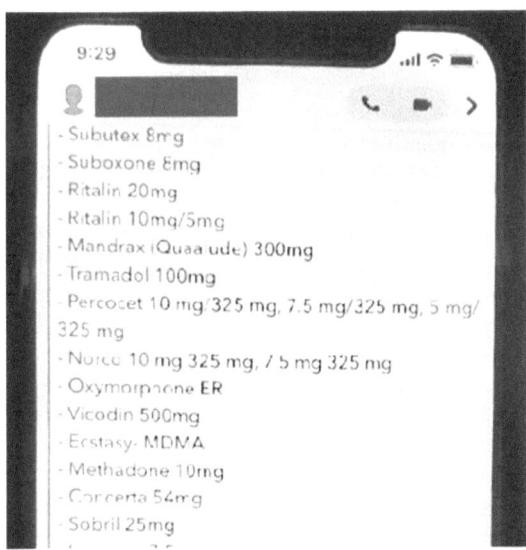

The Organization of Social Media Safety also reports a recent explosion in the supply of fentanyl and other lethal opioids. Combine this with the ease of getting drugs via social media, and we have a recipe for disaster. Overdose deaths are up almost 30 percent, setting historical records, with the trend moving in the wrong direction. To date, social media companies have not been able to stop the sale of drugs on their platforms. Drug dealers communicate using emojis to fool content moderators. Dealers set up fake profiles designed to look like small businesses. Below is an illustration of some of the emojis used.

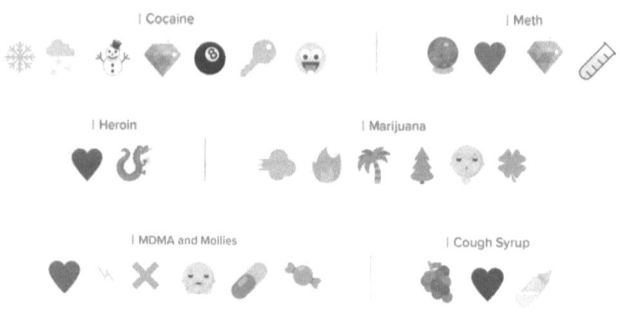

Here are some tips from the Organization of Social Media Safety to protect your child:

- **Have your social media safety conversations.** Discuss the danger of purchasing items from strangers or shady businesses on social media. These products, including prescription drugs, nutritional supplements, and diet pills, can and often will be counterfeit or tainted. Talk to your child about the dangers of substance abuse, especially the newer danger of fentanyl poisoning. While taking unprescribed prescription drugs is never safe, children need to realize that the dangers of taking social media-purchased prescription drugs have increased significantly. With fentanyl circulating, taking any of these drugs, including Vicodin, Xanax, and Percocet, now has a greater risk of death.

- **Set your social media safety rules.** Make sure you tell your child that your family has a rule against using drugs, including unprescribed prescription drugs. While this may seem too obvious to spend time discussing, clearly communicating it to your child increases the likelihood of compliance.

- **Calibrate your social media safety settings.** For tweens and younger teens, ensure your child cannot download social media apps without your permission. Certain apps, like Snapchat, are, in the opinion of The Organization of Social Media Protection, riskier for younger children and have been linked to drug dealing activity. Your child should only be using social media apps that you have judged to be safe, given their current level of maturity and judgment. Ensure your child's social media apps have the maximum privacy setting engaged so drug dealers cannot target and contact them. Consider third-party safety software, which will provide alerts when dangerous content, including drug-related material, comes through your child's social media accounts. This software is recommended for high-risk children, those with a history of substance abuse, behavioral problems, school problems, or mental health issues. Bark is endorsed as an option. While some platforms, like Snapchat, block Bark on iOS, you can use Bark on Android with a lot of these platforms.

Visit the links below for more information on drug dealing and social media.

https://www.socialmediasafety.org/blog/social-media-drugs-what-parents-need-to-know/

https://www.fox28spokane.com/moody-drug-dealers-using-social-media-to-target-minors/

Challenge Discussion #9: Sex and Gender Identity

This section is written by my contributing editor and work colleague, MarDee Rosen Hall, MA, LP.

The birds, the bees, and the penguins!

Like it or not, our children are exposed to sex and sexuality at a very young age from various sources. Typically, during adolescence, when puberty occurs, young people begin to explore their sexuality. However, because of internet exposure like TikTok, YouTube, Instagram, Twitter, etc., that will happen earlier for many. I remember being six years old and getting the birds and bees talk from my mom. She gave me what I could handle and answered questions I had from eavesdropping on the older kids. This first talk established an openness and trust so that, as I got older and had more questions, I could go to her and get honest answers. When she didn't know the answers, she would do research or point me to someone who could provide me with the information I needed. Likewise, with this section, we are not experts and cannot give you all the answers you may need. But we will provide some basics and point you in the direction of other resources that will be helpful to you. Because, believe us, you're going to need it!

The "simple" talk about the birds and the bees—where babies come from, premarital sex, masturbation (it's normal and healthy, by the way), STDs, and birth control—is extremely important and shouldn't be just one talk but a series of short conversations that take place as your kids grow and develop. Why? Because kids are exposed to and expected by their peers to know about all these things at a very sophisticated level. They may be subjected to ridicule or abuse if they don't know. They may also be pressured to have sex—protected or unprotected—before they're emotionally prepared to handle it.

Many parents have the mistaken belief that if they talk openly about these things with their children, they will be putting ideas in their heads or condoning certain behaviors. That is an incorrect assumption. We are not suggesting that you change your religion or run out and buy condoms and birth control for your kids so they can explore sex. We are saying that you need to have honest conversations about sex with your kids and allow them to express their feelings and ask questions. Because if you don't, they will find information from other (and possibly unreliable) sources. We've attached a list of resources at the end of this section, but we thought it pertinent to list the basic dos and don'ts when talking about the birds and bees with your kids. This list comes from the website https://www.choosingtherapy.com/talk-to-kids-about-sex/.

The Dos

When talking with your child about sex, do the following:

- Use direct and clear communication, even if it feels uncomfortable.
- Tailor your conversation based on your child's age and maturity level.
- Explain sexual abuse and encourage them to talk to you about anything that makes them uncomfortable.
- Share your own experiences with going through puberty.
- Talk about safe sex practices.
- Offer resources to your child on puberty and sex, such as books, websites, and pamphlets.
- Encourage them to ask you questions and process their reactions to this information.

The Don'ts

When having a conversation about sex with your child, *don't:*

- Use slang terms for reproductive body parts.
- Shame children for masturbating or being curious about their bodies.
- Discourage children from asking questions.
- Make up answers. If you are unsure about a child's question, you could look up the answer together or let them know you don't know, and you'll follow up with them when you have an answer.
- Be afraid to seek out information or guidance from a healthcare provider, educator, or other reliable sources.

And now for the penguins.

According to a *CNN* article by Scottie Andrew, on February 17, 2022, "The percentage of adults who told Gallup they identify as LGBTQ+ has doubled since 2012, per the polling firm, from 3.5% of Americans to 7.1% of Americans in 2021." The Williams Institute reports that those in the US who identify as transgender are between 0.05 percent and 0.07 percent of the US population. The chance of your child being in the LGBTQ+ category is small. Nevertheless, the numbers are increasing dramatically. This is not because of a fad, peer pressure, or "grooming" by others. There have always been LGBTQ+ children and adults. It's just that now, there is more support for them. Hence, more of them are coming out in the open. John Oliver recently likened this phenomenon to a chart on "handedness."

There was a time when left-handed persons were referred to as "sinister," and left-handedness was discouraged to an extreme—even considered a punishable offense by some. Then, in about 1940, there was a dramatic spike in the population; left-handedness went from 6 percent to 12 percent and then leveled off. This was because people began to accept left-handedness as normal and allowed people to be/express who they truly were. Nowadays, it's hardly even a noticeable thing. Most people are right-handed, but it's understood and accepted that some people are not. It's also understood that left-handedness is not contagious or evil, and left-handed people are not trying to force right-handers to use their other hand. The same is true with the LGBTQ+ population. The population increases as acceptance and support become more available to that community. Consequently, if your kids are not in that group, they will certainly know (or be related to) someone who is.

Here's a little personal story: In my family, both my children told my husband and me early in their adolescence that they were bisexual. Their dad and I told them that that was fine with us, but we believed they were too young to handle the complex emotions that came with having sex. We encouraged abstinence until age eighteen but made sure they knew about birth control. We also provided rules, limits, and supervision when they had company over. At some point, our oldest child began expressing that "he" preferred to use and be referred to by gender-neutral pronouns of "they" and "them." Sometime later, our second child expressed this wish as well. As parents, this was a pretty steep learning curve for us. I assumed it was a "phase" and would go away eventually. As I listened and learned more, I realized that this was not a phase but a journey for both of my children. And that I could be supportive and go along on the journey or be resistant and get left behind. After some wrestling with "what would other people think" and various other societal judgments, I concluded that my greatest wish for my children is that they are happy and fulfilled. For this to happen, I need to support them, no matter what. It's been several years now, it was not a phase, and I'm still learning. My children's lives are much different than I had envisioned for them. They are not married, living in the suburbs, with doctorates or law degrees, and providing us with grandchildren. They are artists and soul seekers who hang out with other nonbinary companions and live very nontraditional but wonderful, fulfilled lives.

According to The Trevor Project, suicide is the second leading cause of death among young people aged ten to twenty-four—and lesbian, gay, bisexual, transgender, queer, and questioning youth are at *significantly increased* risk (Hedegaard, Curtin, & Warner, 2018). LGBTQ+ youth are more than four times as likely to attempt suicide than their peers (Johns et al., 2019; Johns et al., 2020). LGBTQ+ youth are not inherently prone to suicide risk because of their sexual orientation or gender identity but rather placed at higher risk because of how they are mistreated and stigmatized in society.

As a parent, you must ask yourself this very important question: *Would you rather have a depressed/miserable kid, an absent kid, a dead kid, or a happy LGBTQ+ kid?* Because that's what it boils down to. If you don't accept and encourage your children, you won't have them anymore. It's like the story from Emily Kingsley of the mother who thought she was going to Italy—dreamed of it all her life—and then ended up in Holland. It's a shock, maybe a disappointment at first, but after a while, you begin to realize that Holland has many lovely qualities, and if you stop thinking about what your friends are going to say because you spent your time in Holland instead of Italy, you can have a wonderful trip!

Below are some tips from the PA Parent and Family Alliance for talking with your kids about LGBTQ+ issues.

WHAT TO DO AS SOON AS YOUR CHILD COMES OUT TO YOU?

- There will be things you don't know; don't panic. Tell them you will learn what you don't know and be there for every step of their self-discovery.
- Tell them they are in charge of who they come out to and when they decide to do that.
- Reassure them you are always on their side.
- Let them know this only changes what they want it to change.
- Remember, this is the same child you loved yesterday and last week. Continue to love them as you always have.
- They may not be asking you to understand. They are asking you to accept and love them. Don't panic, and let them get their thoughts out before you ask questions.
- If you tell them anything in that moment, back it up with actions. If you tell them you will find them a therapist to talk to, find one. If you tell them you will research, start it that night.

Books:

Where Did I Come From?: An Illustrated Children's Book on Human Sexuality January 1, 1973, by Peter Mayle (Author), Arthur Robins (Illustrator) Lyle Stuart Inc. Publisher

Sex Education for 8-12-Year-Olds: How to Have "The Talk" Without Getting Embarrassed August 11, 2022, by Gerald Mannes (Author) Tomokai River Publisher

Talking with Teens about Sexuality: Critical Conversations about Social Media, Gender Identity, Same-Sex Attraction, Pornography, Purity, Dating, Etc. February 16, 2021, by Robinson (Author) Bethany House Publishers

Helpful Links:

https://www.glaad.org/resources

https://www.npr.org/2019/12/12/787466794/the-birds-and-the-bees-how-to-talk-to-children-about-sex

https://www.todaysparent.com/family/parenting/age-by-age-guide-to-talking-to-kids-about-sex/

https://www.plannedparenthood.org/learn/parents/tips-talking

https://pflag.org/

Challenge Discussion #10: Race Conscious Parenting

Being a Minnesota resident, with an office not ten miles from Chicago Avenue and Thirty-Eighth street in Minneapolis, the scene of the George Floyd murder, I will never forget the day or the impact of the trauma. Walt Jacobs, former chair of the African American & African Studies department at the University of Minnesota, commented in an article about how the George Floyd murder has challenged the notion of "Minnesota nice." *Minnesota nice* is a term used to describe people who prefer discussing surface issues rather than bigger issues that may be divisive, like racism. "You are expected to be polite and not have any hostility to folks who are different than you, and you don't get to know people outside your immediate circle of family and friends."

Jacobs further commented that since Chauvin's conviction, ordinary Minnesotans are starting to have conversations. This is true of my company, which started monthly anti-racism and affinity groups shortly after the George Floyd murder. We are a mostly White mental health agency working within a White mental health system. We are challenged on an ongoing basis to have hard conversations with each other about internalized and systemic racism. It is important for us to be aware, especially White parents, that although we may be well-meaning about racial injustice and wanting to help our kids, we all have blind areas and certain biases that come from our experiences of growing up and developing in predominantly White systems, structures, and spaces. For me, it has been a journey of looking inside myself, acknowledging the impact racism has had on others, and striving to find a way to make an impact on a societal level. Although this section is potentially flawed, being written by a privileged White male, I am grateful to have a company and book that can hopefully be a platform for education and change.

Being a White parent, I have been guilty of avoiding hard conversations about race and racism with my kids. In her book *Raising White Kids: Bringing Up Children in a Racially Unjust America*, Jennifer Harvey writes, "We cannot not see race." Avoiding hard conversations with our children is a disservice to them. For good outcomes, racial development—like physical, intellectual, or emotional development—requires attention from parents and caregivers. White children who are not given opportunities to talk about race fall behind their peers of color whose parents have had "the talk" with them at a young age to help keep them safe. The talk refers to educating a Black child on what to do or not to do when approached by the police. On a larger level, it refers to how race impacts treatment in criminal justice systems. Ibram X Kendi, in his book, *How to Raise an Antiracist*, stresses the importance of parents needing to get past their fear of making mistakes when talking about race with children, stating, "To be a parent is to be imperfect. To be a parent is to be human." When we avoid conversations about race for fear of making mistakes, we run the risk of our kids getting information from racist sources. If your child raises a question about race that you don't know how to respond to, Kendi encourages us to be open about it and willing to explore answers together, using exploration to help kids develop critical thinking skills and empathy, which increases our chances of raising an anti-racist child.

As you may be aware by now, emotional intelligence is at the heart of this book and is a core component of raising a mentally fit child. In a nutshell, emotional intelligence helps children identify how they are feeling, understand the experiences of others, and develop empathy. Emotional intelligence does not end with feeling sad, angry, guilty, or remorseful about what others are experiencing. Dr. Goleman refers to the term "empathic concern," which turns empathy into taking action—doing something about it. This is essentially the same as race-conscious parenting and teaches our kids how to navigate a racially diverse world. Goleman also talks about social neuroscience. We are aware that we have strong unseen and unheard neurological connections when we encounter each other.

Much like a Bluetooth connection, our brains synchronize on a primal level; we make split-second decisions on how to interact. Similarly, Jennifer Harvey comments on how we feel and live race in our bodies, not just in our minds and words. We can have positive ideas, beliefs, and thoughts about racial harmony, but when we encounter each other, "our bodies give us away, every time, and will either create a connection or make it worse." Brain plasticity is another term from Goleman's work. By practicing social skills, in this context, interracial social skills, we build and strengthen pathways in the brain for successful execution. According to Harvey, we need to seek out spaces where our children have the experience of being the minority and participate with humility and openness. This type of practice or exposure can create a congruence between positive ideas, beliefs, and thoughts about racial harmony and feeling it on a deep, authentic (in the bones) level as our children interact with others different from them.

Parents, here are some tips from Embrace Race for teaching and talking to kids about race consciousness:

- **Start early.** By six months, babies start noticing racial differences; by age four, children begin to show signs of racial bias. Let your child know it is perfectly okay to notice skin color and discuss race. Talk about what racial differences mean and don't mean.

- **Encourage your child.** Encourage your child to ask questions, share observations and experiences, and be respectfully curious about race. Expose your child to different cultural opportunities, photographs, films, books, or cultural events. Be honest about what you don't know, and work with your child to find accurate information.

- **Be mindful.** You are a role model to your child. What you say is important, but what you do and the diversity of your friendship circle is likely to have a bigger impact. If your child doesn't attend a diverse school, consider after-school or weekend activities that include persons of different races and ethnicities. Visit museums with exhibits about a range of cultures and religions.

- **Face and know your own bias.** Let your child see you acknowledge and face your own biases. We are less likely to pass on the biases we identify and work to overcome. Give your child an example of a bias, racial or otherwise, that you hold or have held. Share what you do to confront and overcome that bias.

- **Know and live who you are.** Talk about the histories and experiences of racial, ethnic, and cultural groups you and your family identify with. Talk about their contributions and acknowledge the less flattering parts of those histories as well. Tell stories about the challenges your family (your child's parents, aunts and uncles, grandparents, and great-grandparents) has faced and overcome.

- **Develop racial and cultural literacy.** Study and talk about the histories and experiences of groups we call African Americans, Latinos, Asian Americans, Native Americans, and

Whites, among others. Be sure your child understands that every racial and ethnic group includes people who believe different things and behave differently. There is as much diversity within racial groups as across them.

- **Be honest.** Be honest with your child in age-appropriate ways about bigotry and oppression. Children are amazing at noticing patterns, including racial patterns—for example, who lives in their neighborhoods versus their friends' neighborhoods. Help them make sense of those patterns and recognize that bigotry and oppression are sometimes a big part of those explanations. Be sure your child knows that the struggle for racial fairness is still happening and that your family can take part in that struggle.

- **Tell stories.** Tell stories of resistance and resilience. Every big story of racial oppression is also a story about people fighting back and "speaking truth to power." Teach your child those parts of the story too. Include women, children, and young adults among the "freedom fighters" in the stories you tell. A story about racial struggle in which all the heroes are men wrongly leaves many people out.

- **Be active.** Be active; don't be a "bystander" on race. Help your child understand what it means to be a change agent. Whenever possible, connect the conversations you're having to the change you and your child want to see and ways to bring about that change.

- **Plan for a marathon, not a sprint.** It's okay to say, "I'm not sure," or "Let's come back to that later, okay?" But then do come back to it. Make race talks with your child routine. Race is a topic you should plan to revisit again and again in many different ways.

Check out the links below for more resources on raising racially conscious children:

https://tinkergarten.com/blog/17-resources-to-help-parents-raise-anti-racist-kids

https://healthblog.uofmhealth.org/childrens-health/raising-race-conscious-children-how-to-talk-to-kids-about-race-and-racism

https://centerracialjustice.org/resources/resources-for-talking-about-race-racism-and-racialized-violence-with-kids/

https://www.pbs.org/education/blog/10-tips-on-talking-to-kids-about-race-and-racism

https://www.kurtzpsychology.com/cultivating-race-consciousness-by-talking-to-children-about-race-and-racism/

https://myips.org/get-involved/racial-equity/resource-guide-for-white-teachers-parents-developing-racial-consciousness-and-moving-into-action/

https://www.mother.ly/parenting/raising-race-conscious-children/

https://www.rti.org/insights/parenting-race-conscious-lens

Chapter 6 Assignment:

Review each of these topics and think about your concerns for your child. Prioritize them in terms of importance to you and your family. Address the most important ones first by using the tips provided in each section. Take notes in your journal and revisit them later to monitor progress.

CHAPTER 7:

Step 4—Design an Alliance

Relationship Is Everything!

YOUR RELATIONSHIP WITH your child is more important than how skilled you are at coaching them. In the fields of mental health and coaching, it is well established that the relationship between therapist or coach and client is what keeps them engaged and moving forward. A therapist or coach can have all the credentials in the world and fail miserably if they don't know how to connect with their client. Sometimes parents get frustrated with me in my work with their teens. Their child will tell them something like, "I like Dr. Hoy; we have some good talks, and sometimes we play games." Then, I might receive a phone call from an angry dad who says something like, "My kid can play games anywhere. Why am I paying for this?" I explain that I have a variety of ways to connect with kids to gain trust so they can do the work.

Christopher was a fifteen-year-old client who came to me a few years ago. He was struggling greatly in school and at home. He had gone through several therapists prior to seeing me. His parents reported that he simply wouldn't talk with other therapists about his problems. He had a very short attention span and struggled with doing schoolwork, completing chores, and following basic household rules. His parents punished him by grounding him in his room and taking the things he most cared about from him. He loved music and had formed a small garage band with some kids from the neighborhood.

However, his parents took away any access to music, practice time with friends, radio, television, computer, cell phones, and his guitar. This was an example of authoritarian parenting gone awry. The more his parents tried to control his behavior through harsh punishment, the more withdrawn, sullen, and defiant Christopher became. Our first few sessions were challenging to say the least.

From his perspective, I was just another adult trying to tell him what to do. He responded to my inquiries with one-word answers, shrugs, and grunts. I had to find a different way to communicate with him. I asked him what bothered him the most about his parents. "They're always taking away my music!" he blurted. This gave me a clue about how to connect with him. I began to engage him in discussions about music. He came alive and educated me on a variety of different genres. I learned the difference between pop, hip-hop, and rap. We began showing each other music videos we liked on my computer. This was the beginning of our alliance. After a few weeks, I introduced structure and limits to our sessions. I explained that while I enjoyed him and the music, we had some work to do. By that point, we had established enough trust and safety in our relationship that he was willing to negotiate with me. We then came to an agreement: he could play a song he liked at the beginning and the end of the session, and in between, he would talk about things he was struggling with, like grades, school, and his frustration with his parents. Eventually, he brought music into the sessions that related to his life. That's when things really began to turn around for him.

In a sense, it was easier for me than his parents to establish an alliance with this young man. I had no history with him. On the other hand, his parents had a history of conflicts and power struggles going back several years. They had significant work to do around repairing relationship damage and reestablishing their alliance. To facilitate this, I met with the parents separately. I began by validating their efforts and frustrations. I assured them that I knew how difficult it is to raise teens. I had them share photo albums of them as a family. I asked them to tell me what their happiest moments were with Christopher. As they shared stories about their son, they softened and were much more open about their feelings. They connected with their deep love for him and identified that behind their anger was worry and fear for his future. As I got to know them better and they became more comfortable with me, they shared some of their shortcomings and struggles. We laughed about how, sometimes, as parents, we need to get over ourselves. They realized they had high expectations for Christopher and that much of their fear was about not wanting to look bad as parents. I then led them into a discussion of what they liked about Christopher and what his strengths were. "He can be really affectionate, and he has a good sense of humor," said Dad. Mom added that he was a good musician. This opened Dad up to talk about his love of music and how he could identify with Christopher. I shared with Dad how I had connected with Christopher in sessions around music and encouraged him to do the same.

We were then ready to meet as a family. I facilitated a dialogue between Christopher and his parents, wherein they could take responsibility for the past mistakes they had made with him. As his parents modeled this behavior, Christopher became less defiant and began to take responsibility for his own mistakes. This cleaned the slate and set the stage for a new beginning. It was like hitting a "reset" button. From there, I led Christopher's parents into "rally" mode. I pointed out that the next few years were an opportunity for them to really have a huge impact on his future and their long-term relationship with him. I coached them to think of themselves as cheerleaders first and disciplinarians second. This perspective shift was transformational for them. They became energized and began redirecting their efforts toward what was going right in his life. Unchained from their rigid expectations for him, they became excited about the possibility of moving forward. They went to his neighborhood pickup softball games. Dad occasionally substituted for players who couldn't make the games while Mom brought her foldout chair and sat on the sidelines, cheering them on. Christopher's parents allowed him to invite his bandmates to their garage for practice. Eventually, the band invited Dad to sit in on a session, and he taught them a Ramones song!

Although we made good progress, we weren't out of the woods. There were still disciplinary issues; Christopher was only fifteen years old. I educated his parents on the parenting styles previously outlined in chapter five. I coached them to adopt the authoritative style as opposed to the authoritarian style they had been using. They continued to maintain high standards for school attendance and behavior without "keeping him down" with harsh punishment. Christopher was given space to bounce around, make mistakes, and learn from natural consequences within a container of safety created by his parents. When Christopher overslept and missed a class, his parents encouraged him to talk with his teacher about how to make up the class instead of grounding him and taking away his music. His teacher required him to come to school on a Saturday morning and write a short paper on the topic of the class he missed. When natural consequences weren't readily available, they used logical ones.

For example, when Christopher came home an hour past curfew on a Friday evening, his parents made him come in an hour earlier the next time he went out. As for his homework, Christopher's mom began checking the school app every week, and if he had assignments missing, she would take him to her office on Saturdays. While she caught up on her paperwork, Christopher worked on his assignments. They would then take a break and have lunch together and discuss what he'd been working on, and she would praise him for his efforts. Sometimes they would take in a movie at the end of the day as a reward for his hard work. Gradually, Christopher began to experience more success in school. Success led to increased confidence and internal motivation. "It's so nice not to have to feel like I'm nagging him all the time," Mom said to me. At this point, the family was able to graduate from therapy.

Most of the case studies I have shared with you are more on the extreme side. Your situation may not be as intense or have all the elements of Christopher's or Jack's. However, designing an alliance with your child is the same regardless of your situation. You need to take responsibility for your past mistakes without feeling like a failure as a parent, clean the slate, establish trust and safety in your relationship, identify a shared goal, and think of yourself as a cheerleader first and disciplinarian second.

Taking Responsibility and Cleaning the Slate

Nobody's perfect; we all make mistakes. When my son was fifteen, he told me he felt demoralized by my yelling. Consequently, I felt intense guilt and sadness. I had to take a hard look at my behavior. I realized that, in response to his normal adolescent shenanigans, I had become controlling, unreasonable, and rigid. I took his behavior as an affront to my authority. A little voice in my head said, "Not *my* son—what will other people think of me?" I was so focused on myself and how I looked as a parent that I wasn't attuned to my son's needs. I was missing the big picture! My son's entire world was expanding—sports, girls, music, large classes, more homework, hormonal changes, and peer pressure. Rather than yell and try to control him, he needed me to walk beside him and help him navigate. His behavior was not about me. It was not an affront; it was a call to action. When I finally figured it out, I acknowledged my mistakes and apologized.

Trust & Safety

In my early work with Christopher, I intentionally created a safe space for him and developed trust. I led with authenticity. I was genuinely interested in him, and he knew it. I listened much more than I talked. Although his parents had given me a large laundry list of complaints, I didn't judge, criticize, or tell him what to do. I let him know what he could expect of me. I would be honest and show up every week. And if a problem arose with scheduling, I would call him and let him know. I set parameters. For example, we could have music at the beginning and end of our sessions, with problem discussions in the middle. I respected his pace and didn't try to push him to talk about issues he wasn't ready to address. After you clean the slate with your child, you will need to establish trust and safety.

Identify a Shared Goal

After cleaning the slate and establishing trust and safety, our next task was to work on a shared goal. When I met with Christopher individually and asked him about his goals for the next few years, he replied, "I want to have my own car and have the freedom to go and hang out with my friends." He wanted to be able to get some paid "gigs" on the weekends with his bandmates. "I want to get a dorm room at the University of Minnesota with my three best buds and study music. And I want a girlfriend." When I met with his parents and asked them what their goals for Christopher were for the next few years, Dad said, "He needs to get his grades up so he can get into a good business school." His mother wanted him to get into a profession where he could make enough money to live on his own and support a family. They were focused more on security, whereas Christopher's primary focus was on freedom.

Christopher and his parents were truly deadlocked in a power struggle. Have you ever been involved in sports with your child? If so, you are probably aware of how crazy some parents get when they watch their kids play. We absolutely lose all objectivity. It's understandable because of how much we love our kids. "Why isn't my kid pitching? He's the best out there. She should be playing more! She's getting a raw deal! I'm going to talk to that coach!" Many parents who have kids in sports played the same sport themselves when they were in high school. It is very common for us to want our kids to do better than we did. Unfortunately, "wants" can become expectations, and expectations can become demands. "You will make the varsity hockey team! You will not miss any practices! You will keep your grades up." The unintended consequence of our deep love for our children can create a disconnect between our goals for them and their goals for themselves, resulting in a deadlock.

I brought Christopher and his parents in for a family session. I had each of them write down goals on sticky notes and put them up on my wall. I added some levity to the process by using many different colored sticky notes and encouraging them to dream big. I instructed them to do the exercise for fifteen minutes nonstop and write down absolutely everything that came to mind. By the end of the fifteen minutes, my office wall had become a brightly-colored collage of hopes and wishes. From that collage, we identified two major themes: freedom and security. We grouped the sticky notes into these two categories on the wall. My job was to validate the importance of both themes. I educated Christopher's parents on how freedom and independence are very appropriate goals for a young man his age. I explained to Christopher that it was his parent's job to guide him, and sometimes that involves setting limits and having expectations. I then drew two intersecting circles on the paper, with one circle representing freedom and the other representing security. I had them determine which of their notes fit in the middle, where the circles intersected, representing both security and freedom. The negotiations began. Christopher wanted music, and his dad wanted business. The shared goals were that both parties valued higher education, financial independence, and social connections. I explained to Christopher's parents that passion creates movement, which is key to Christopher's motivation. When he gets into college, he may find something else he is passionate about and change his major. He may even find out that business is his passion. The point is that his parents needed to give him room to explore and learn independently.

Cheerleader First/Disciplinarian Second

In a private session with Christopher's parents, I told them, "It's like you have to be a cheerleader first and a disciplinarian second." Mom then brightened and said, "I was a cheerleader in high school!" I asked Mom to give me a job description for a cheerleader. She explained,

"You must be able to create excitement with the fans for the team. You never lose faith, even when they are losing." She spoke about the importance of cheer. You must cheer your team on and stay positive. I talked with Mom about how I would grimace in high school, watching the cheerleaders flip across the field and land into the splits. Mom said, "Oh, yeah, we did all of that stuff."

"In other words," I said, "you had to be very flexible."

"Yes . . . for sure!" she exclaimed. I drew an analogy between cheerleading on a sports team and cheerleading for your child. I encouraged them to be excited for him and never lose faith, even when he is having a bad day. I coached them to praise him more for his efforts than the outcome and to celebrate any and every victory, no matter how small. Above all, I underscored the importance of being flexible and willing to bend.

Freedom to move and explore is very important for our teen children. However, it is crucial for parents to provide a safe container in which to do so. When working with parents to convey this message, I have them remember their child learning to walk and move about as a toddler. They take off, stop, look back at you, and decide whether to run to you or continue. It can be perilous. Sometimes they fall. This is a natural consequence of exploration. Often, you must swoop in and rescue them from danger, like falling down a flight of stairs or sticking a finger in a light socket. You may have to discipline them to keep them safe. This is how we provide containment for our toddlers. When children become teenagers, they revisit this stage in many ways. They need to explore and experiment with new behaviors. Sometimes it is perilous. "Falling" for a teenager might look like getting detention for clowning around in the classroom or being embarrassed by a Snapchat post. These are examples of natural consequences. Sometimes, you must swoop in and rescue them from danger, like going to parties, hanging out with older kids, and experimenting with alcohol. You may have to discipline them to keep them safe.

As discussed in chapter five, authoritative parenting has been found to produce the best results for kids. As you are designing an alliance with your child, let them know that you are adopting a coaching style that you have learned will help them get what they want. This way, they will know you are working for their success instead of trying to control them. If their grades are down, let them know that they can expect you to set limits on leisure activities. As they get back on track, you will ease up and allow them to spend time on other things they like to do. Set high expectations for school attendance and negotiate the use of social media. Work with them to avoid using their devices while studying (unless they are doing schoolwork). Rather than continually asking about grades and the status of assignments, shoot for a check-in time once per week that you both agree upon. Encourage them to get a job. Part-time work for teens has been found to improve grades because it helps kids get into a rhythm and stay on schedule. Ask them what they need from you to help them improve school performance. Do your best to set up a home environment conducive to learning. Remember, praising them for their effort is more effective than an outcome, such as getting a good grade on a test.

Sometimes, as parents, we put the cart before the horse and try to get to the end goal too quickly. Building a strong alliance takes patience. Think of it as a process, not an event. Take time to make time. If you are unable to maintain a strong alliance with your child throughout this process, they will not be on board with you. A great way to connect is to find something they like and take a genuine interest in it with them.

You can expect that you will get some pushback. That's what kids do. If you feel stressed when they push back, they will feel the same way. Being stressed out all the time reduces our ability to problem-solve. Try your best to avoid power struggles, and choose your battles. If you get deadlocked on something and emotions run high, I recommend moving on to something else. Make sure you are fully present when you meet. Be authentic. When setbacks occur, and you can expect they will, focus on what you can do to move forward instead of spending most of your time on what didn't work. You can certainly build some fun into this process. Negotiate activities you can do together as rewards, like going out to movies or having meals together. And whatever you do, don't give up. You are in this one-hundred-percent.

Chapter 7 Assignment:

Gather multicolored sticky notes and meet with your child. Take fifteen minutes to dream big and write down as many goals for your child as possible. Have your child do the same for himself/herself. Find common themes, group them together, and determine where the intersection is. Identify one, two, or three shared goals to be allied around moving forward.

CHAPTER 8:

Step 5—Lay a Solid Foundation

GOOD JOB! YOU have designed an alliance with your child. Let's make sure we have our feet under us. In this chapter, I will talk about the importance of foundational skills, not only for your child's success in life but for the overall health of their generation. I am aware that you most likely know a great deal about time and money management, nutrition, sleep, and physical activity. However, just because we *know* what we need doesn't mean we always *do* what we need. We stock our houses with healthy foods, provide comfy beds and an alarm clock, put a trampoline in the backyard and a basketball hoop in the driveway, and expect our kids to do the rest. The truth is that they are neither sleeping, exercising, eating right, nor managing their time effectively. A record number of our internet-generation kids are in crisis. They are distracted and ignoring critical foundational needs. Most of the distraction they are experiencing is preventable. At the risk of sounding like my grandfather, we need to get our kids back to the basics!

Time Management

I recently interviewed fifty college students in five focus groups and asked them what they thought was the most stressful part of transitioning from high school to college. The hands-down response was "time management." One of the participants talked about feeling depressed after making a conscious choice to go down the "rabbit hole" of spending all night on her cell phone when she knew she was supposed to be studying. Another one talked about arriving late to class for exams and being so anxious that she couldn't answer the test questions she had studied for. Time management is linked to higher GPAs and has also been shown to lower anxiety and reduce stress by creating a sense of control. Now is the time to get your child on a time management plan. Here are some suggestions for getting started:

- **Time management tools.** Whether it's a planner that your teen writes everything in or an app that manages their schedule, help them find the tools that will work best. Talk about the importance of creating a schedule and using lists to prioritize time wisely.
- **Write down a schedule.** Teach your teen to schedule their day so they can set aside time for chores, homework, physical activity, time away from electronics, and other responsibilities. You can also encourage them to schedule free time.
- **Prioritize activities**. It's common for teens to run into conflicts in their schedules. Teach them how to prioritize activities based on values and commitments.
- **Develop routines**. Encourage your teen to establish routines, like doing chores right after school. Routines help teens stay on track.
- **Set limits on electronics**. Negotiate a plan to help your child create healthy habits with cell phones and other digital devices.
- **Model good time management habits.** Be on time for your child and model punctuality by making it to appointments when scheduled. Demonstrate your ability to use time management habits to balance work, personal time, and family life.

One of the biggest stressors reported by teens coming out of middle school is adjusting to the amount of studying required in high school. And if they choose to go to college, it is even more intense.

Here are some time management study tips to pass on to your child to help them succeed academically:

1. **Take good notes.** Date each entry and keep notes from different classes separate from each other. Write down anything your instructor puts on the board. If the instructor took the time to write it out, they consider it important. Try to take notes in outline form. The organization of ideas is as important as the content, especially when it comes to learning exam material.

2. **Review your notes every day.** Spend thirty minutes each evening going over notes from each class. Research shows that reviewing new material within twenty-four hours of hearing it significantly increases your retention of that material. Review material before each class to identify points of confusion and prepare you for asking questions.

3. **Alternate study locations.** Alternating study spaces is an effective way to retain information. Although you may have a favorite spot to study, research suggests changing locations is better. Memory is influenced by location, so changing your study locale increases the likelihood of remembering what you learned.

4. **Get enough sleep.** Sleep is essential for effective study. When you're tired, you think more slowly and tend not to retain as much information. If you want to get the most out of your study sessions, ensure you get enough sleep.

5. **Use flashcards.** Writing notes and definitions more than once will help imprint information in your memory. Write down important facts for a test and quiz yourself each day until you have mastered the material. Flashcards are convenient because they allow you to condense material and eliminate irrelevant information.

6. **Join a study group.** When working through a difficult problem set or assignment, a study group can prove invaluable. Dividing the work amongst your peers is also an effective method for reducing your workload and ensuring that you understand the material.

7. **Don't immerse yourself in subject matter.** Immersing yourself in a subject for long periods of time is less effective when it comes to memory retention than switching between topics. Take a break from each topic after thirty minutes and move on to another. You can come back to the topic after you have spent some time studying others. When you revisit the topic, you will feel refreshed and ready to pick up where you left off.

8. **Don't wait until the night before an exam to study.** Cramming before an exam causes feelings of desperation and can lead to test anxiety. Instead, jot down a few ideas or facts you want to have fresh in your mind before the test. Read through your list a few times when you get up in the morning and once again just before you take the exam. This kind of memory reinforcement improves your performance on the test and your long-term memory of the material.

9. **College-level study requirements.** In higher education, a well-established rule of thumb holds that students should devote two hours of study time for every hour of class time. Full-time students taking fifteen credits can plan on studying thirty hours per week.

Money Management

According to a recent study published on parents.com, 69 percent of internet-generation kids, or those born between the 1990s and the early 2000s, do not comprehend properly how much they should spend relative to how much they should save for long-term goals. They simply lack the knowledge or skills to make a budget. It is easy to avoid conversations with our kids about money and budgeting; however, it is extremely important. Financial literacy is just as important as the needs mentioned in the bottom two rungs of Maslow's hierarchy for food, water, warmth, sleep, and the need to feel safe and secure. Hence, money management is a very important foundational skill in my mental fitness framework. When engaging your child in discussions about money management, keep conversations short and make them enjoyable. Talk to them about how you manage your money as a family, and if you are able, offer to match their savings or provide other incentives.

Surprise, surprise . . . there are many money management apps to help your teen learn about managing money. The key is to find some that they like and are interested in using. Ideally, you want something engaging, simple, and useful. Here are a few:

- **FamZoo**—the FamZoo family finance app teaches kids how to manage their money by allowing for the creation of accounts that give every dollar a purpose, such as saving, investing, giving, and spending.
- **Savings Spree**—this is an app for kids seven and up. Like FamZoo, it teaches about saving, investing, spending, and giving, however, within a game show format.
- **Bankaroo**—billed as a virtual bank for kids, Bankaroo teaches them how to spend responsibly and save for their long-term goals.

Here are some tips from the Parents Network for helping your teen learn to manage money:

- **Set them up with bank accounts.** Open a checking account for daily spending and a savings account for future goals. For peace of mind, you can open a teen checking account that gives you joint holder status while giving your child the freedom and independence to manage the account online with a smartphone. A debit card connected to the account minimizes the need to carry cash and keeps a record of where the money is spent.

- **Put them in charge.** You may have heard of the fifty/thirty/twenty rule. It is a good way to help teens start thinking about making a budget that works for their current life situation. Fifty percent goes to essentials, thirty percent is for personal spending, and twenty percent goes toward savings. Starting early is a great way to help them learn how to make smart decisions when they move out or go to college.

- **Teach them some insurance basics.** If your teen is close to driving age, explain that the purpose of insurance is to cover big costs that would otherwise be hard to pay on their own. Teach them about deductibles and create skin in the game for safe driving by having them take partial responsibility for accidents they may cause.

- **Create credit smarts.** As scary as it may seem, giving your child a credit card is an opportunity to teach them about the difference between credit and cash and build a credit history. You can start with low-limit teen-friendly cards such as Apple, Journey, Rewards, or Discover. If you are going this route, monitor the account to help protect their credit rating. Explain how interest rates increase the costs of purchases over time.

- **Discuss the economics of higher education.** If your child is moving toward higher education, getting as clear as possible about the costs versus benefits is important. Junior Achievement's JA Build Your Future app helps students crunch the numbers. Students should not have to incur more debt than they can reasonably afford to pay back based on their career interests.

- **Plant a retirement seed:** Let them know that retirement is the biggest expense they will ever have. If they are employed and earning an income, think about opening an individual retirement account (IRA). The earlier they start, the more money they will have, and time is definitely on their side compared to others who have neglected to do so.

Sleep Hygiene

We are a sleep-deprived society. A recent report from the CDC estimated that over one-third of the adult population in the US sleeps less than the recommended minimum of seven hours each night. And teens, who need just over nine hours of sleep a night, are the least likely of any age group to get sufficient rest. According to a survey from the National Sleep Foundation, about 80 percent of American high school students are chronically sleep-deprived. Sleep deprivation has been linked to increases in depression, suicide attempts, and learning and behavior issues in school. Schools have established later start times for children as we became aware that sufficient sleep is linked to higher grades.

The biggest current-day contributors to lack of sleep, as you can probably guess, are electronic devices: cell phones, televisions, MP3 players, texting, and video games. Teenagers naturally have a harder time sleeping at night because of a delay in the release of a hormone, melatonin, which is secreted when it is dark to induce sleep. Sleeping near an electronic device that gives off light delays the release of melatonin. It's like throwing gas on a fire. Your child's sleep is disrupted by staying up late at night, using an electronic device, and sleeping next to it. Below is a snapshot of statistics from a survey done by Michigan Medicine, from the University of Michigan, which polled parents about teen sleep disruption.

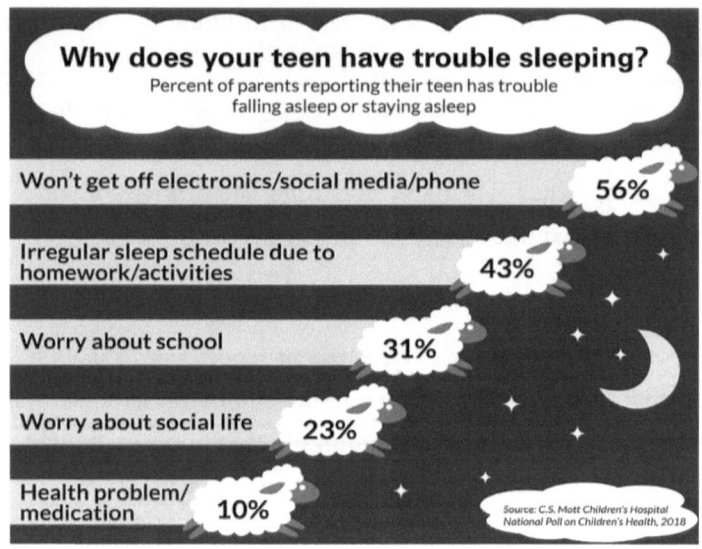

Fifty-six percent of parents reported teen sleep deprivation due to electronics and social media use. Forty-three percent attributed irregular sleep to homework requirements and other activities, such as sports. Thirty-one percent said their kids often lay awake at night worrying about school. Twenty-three percent reported that their kids stayed up worrying about social lives, and ten percent cited health problems as a cause for disrupted sleep. Below are suggestions to help your teen have a better sleep:

- **Ban electronics from the bedroom.** Use of electronics, including social media and cellphones, is the top reason parents cite for their teens' sleep troubles.
- **Charge cell phones elsewhere.** Make it a family rule to charge all devices in an isolated space to reduce temptation at bedtime. Many teens feel relieved when their parents limit phone use because it removes some of the pressure to keep up with peers on social media.
- **Maintain a regular sleep schedule.** Keeping a sleep schedule within an hour of what's usual helps to keep the sleep cycle in

check. Sleeping late on weekends doesn't make up for lost sleep.
- **Discourage afternoon naps.** Naps make it harder to fall asleep at night.
- **Don't procrastinate on big tasks.** Encourage getting homework done as soon as teens get home from school or negotiate a short break before they begin.
- **Stick to sleep-friendly bedtime routines.** All stimulation should be minimized. Keep the lights low and active pets out of the bedroom. Some kids like to use music to relax and wind down; however, this may keep their brains stimulated.
- **Limit caffeine.** Discourage energy drinks, which tend to have much higher levels of caffeine than tea or coffee. Discourage the use of caffeinated drinks later than lunchtime to prevent sleep disruption.
- **Talk with your doctor about melatonin.** Teens naturally have a harder time sleeping at night. Melatonin as a supplement may be helpful.

Nutrition

Just as sleep has been proven to help teens get better grades, so has attention to proper nutrition. Eating breakfast each morning has positive effects on brain function. Kids who eat breakfast have better concentration during school hours than those who skip morning meals. Nationally, 60 percent of American teens skip eating breakfast daily. According to pediatrician Dr. William Sears, children who eat breakfast in the morning before school participate more in classroom discussions, are better able to handle complex problems, and get better grades. A breakfast meal containing a balance of protein and complex carbohydrates makes your child's brain alert and boosts school performance throughout the day.

Examples of good sources of protein are

- Eggs in moderation
- Cheese
- Peanut butter
- Lean meats, fish, and poultry
- Lentils and other legumes
- Nuts and seeds
- Protein-fortified foods like cereals

Here are some basic daily protein guidelines for children:

- Children ages nine to thirteen: thirty-four grams
- Girls ages fourteen to eighteen: forty-six grams
- Boys ages fourteen to eighteen: fifty-two grams

Healthy complex carbohydrate choices include:

- **Whole grains.** These are good sources of fiber. At most grocery stores, you can find whole-grain versions of rice, bread, cereal, flour, and pasta. Many whole-grain foods, including a variety of bread, pasta, and cereals, are ready to eat.
- **Fiber-rich fruits.** Apples, berries, bananas, oranges, and strawberries are good fiber-rich choices. Avoid canned fruit since it usually contains added syrup.
- **Fiber-rich vegetables.** Potatoes, broccoli, carrots, collard greens, spinach (and other leafy greens), green beans, and asparagus.
- **Beans.** Navy beans are one of the richest sources of fiber. Other fiber-rich sources include pinto beans, black beans, split peas, lentils, mung beans, adzuki beans, and lima beans.

Suggestions for a healthy breakfast:

- Oatmeal with fruits and nuts

- Higher calcium, lower-fat dairy foods
- Whole-grain cereal with dried fruits, nuts, and low-fat milk or soy milk
- Egg breakfasts with a small amount of fat
- High-protein yogurt with fruits
- Whole wheat bread with peanut butter or cheese
- Fruit salad with cottage cheese
- A shake blended with yogurt, milk or soy milk, and fruits

If your teen isn't hungry first thing in the morning, pack a breakfast they can eat a little later, on the bus or between classes, such as fresh fruit, cereal, nuts, or half a peanut butter and banana sandwich. Sandwiches are easy to make and easy for kids to take along and eat later. Teens typically need more calories due to rapid growth and development. Specifically, boys need an average of 2,800 calories per day, while girls need an average of 2,200 calories. If you use protein bars as nutritional choices for your kids, make sure you read the labels for ingredients. Some are rich in nutrients, and some are more like candy bars, with sugars and unhealthy fats. Others contain unnecessary carbohydrates intended for endurance athletes.

We are always hearing about diets and nutrition in the media, so much so that it can be confusing and overwhelming to keep up with. To keep things simple, below are two models for you to consider as you meal plan for your family. In 2011, the USDA replaced the food pyramid with a nutritional guide called "My Plate." It depicts a place setting divided into five food groups: fruits, grains, protein, vegetables, and dairy.

Visit the USDA website (ChooseMyPlate.Gov) with your child to teach them about nutrition, using the plate as a guide for meal planning. The CDC reports that teens consume significantly fewer fruits and vegetables required by dietary guidelines. Girls should eat 1.5 cups of fruit and 2.5 cups of vegetables daily, while boys should eat 2 cups of fruit and 3 cups of vegetables. A cup is the equivalent of one medium-sized apple or eight strawberries. Health care experts are now pondering the addition of water intake to the My Plate guide. National Health and Nutrition Survey statistics indicate that most American teens aren't drinking enough water and are mildly dehydrated. Teens, in general, report drinking little fluids of any kind. Dehydration, even mild, negatively impacts energy level, mood, and learning. Teenagers should consume roughly 2 to 3 quarts or 1.7 to 3.3 liters of water a day.

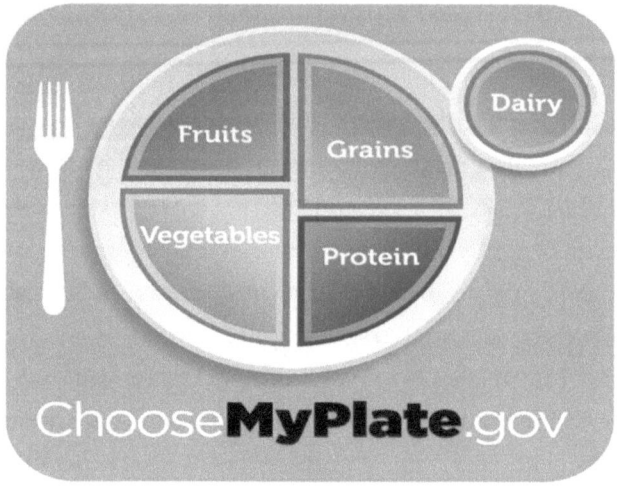

Although the USDA is a highly respected and very good resource for learning about healthy eating, I would like to share some information from Dan Beutner and his work on the Blue Zones Project to help you think about nutrition on a different level. In 2005, he wrote a cover story for *National Geographic*, "The Secrets of Living a Long Life." In his research, he discovered five places in the world named "The Blue Zones," where people lived the longest and were the healthiest: Loma Linda, California; Nicoya, Costa Rica; Sardinia, Italy; Icaria, Greece, and Okinawa, Japan. Many of them are described as "centenarian" locations due to their population living to one hundred years old and beyond. Below is a visual aid to help you understand dietary characteristics shared by these very healthy individuals.

The most profound difference between what people in the blue zones eat compared to others around the world is the balance between plant and animal eating—95 percent plant-based versus 5 percent animal-based. That said, the US and other nations are gearing up to be part of the plant-protein industry, which, according to food analysts, will increase from a 4.6-billion-dollar industry in 2018 to 85 billion by 2030. Due to a growing global population of consumers wishing to make more sustainable, health-conscious food choices, this trend has been coming for some time and has been exacerbated by the advent of COVID-19. The emergence of the pandemic has highlighted the importance of a healthy immune system. Additionally, COVID has led people to experiment with plant-based proteins due to animal protein shortages.

It may not be realistic for you to fully implement such a diet for family health; however, there are many resources and cookbooks with healthy options from vegan, solely plant-based food, to vegetarian, excluding meat, poultry, and fish but including other animal products, to flexitarian, eating mainly vegetables, with occasional red meat, poultry, and seafood. For more information on blue zones food guidelines, you can visit the link below.

http://www.bluezones.com/recipes/food-guidelines/

Junk Food

Let's take a minute to talk about junk food. In a 2015 *New York Times* article, the CDC statistics revealed that American teens consume 16.9 percent of their calories from junk food, such as hamburgers, french fries, and pizza. On any given day, researchers calculated that 34.5 percent of children and adolescents, aged two to nineteen years old, take in 25 percent of their calories from junk food. And as you can imagine, junk food consumption leads to obesity. *NBC News*, in an article published in 2023, reported on a government survey and found the prevalence of adult obesity in the US to be 40 percent. The CDC reports US childhood obesity rates for ages two to nineteen years old, from 2017 to 2020, to be 19.7 percent, equating to 14.7 million kids. Severe obesity has become so widespread and dangerous among youths that the American Academy of Pediatrics now recommends that bariatric weight loss surgery be considered a safe treatment option for children and teens. As a health professional, it is disheartening to think that we have reached a point where surgery, once considered a last resort for adults with morbid obesity, has entered the mainstream as an acceptable treatment for young people.

According to a large *US News & World Report* study, there is a positive correlation between watching junk food ads and consuming foods high in salt, sugar, and fat. The bottom line is that kids who watch more ads tend to eat more junk. Here goes my grandpa's voice again: TURN OFF THE TV! GET AWAY FROM THAT COMPUTER! THOSE ADS WILL BRAINWASH YOU!

Fad Diets

Advertisements and social media glorify eating unhealthy foods while at the same time celebrating unrealistic body images. We are barraged by pictures of skinny women and muscular men as ideal body types. Teens searching for identity are particularly susceptible to these messages. To this end, they can become vulnerable to buying into the fad diet craze. Fad diets can be dangerous because they are not balanced or sustainable. Signs of a fad diet are:

- Promise of a huge weight loss in a short period of time. For example, "Drop 10 pounds in one week, guaranteed."
- Claims that the diet works with no exercise needed.
- Certain foods are never allowed.
- Foods are called "good" or "bad."
- Special foods are needed that are hard to find or can only be bought in certain shops.

Eating Disorders

Fad diets can lead to eating disorders among young people. The National Eating Disorder Association (NEDA) has reported that eating disorders have increased steadily since the 1950s. In her book, *Understanding Teen Eating Disorders: Warning Signs, Treatment Options, and Stories of Courage*, Mary Tantillo identifies the following behaviors that may indicate your child is struggling with an eating disorder:

1. BODY INSECURITY: Negative or obsessive thoughts about body size or shape. Persistent worries or complaints about being fat or the need to lose weight.
2. EXCESSIVE EXERCISE: Obsessive about getting daily exercise. Exercises even when injured, tired, or sick.
3. FEAR OF EATING IN FRONT OF OTHERS: Avoids situations that include eating in front of others or in public. Makes excuses about not being able to eat with friends or family.
4. VICARIOUS PLEASURE IN OTHERS' EATING: Prepares elaborate meals for others but rarely eats what is made.
5. CHANGES IN APPEARANCE: Significant loss, gain, or fluctuation in weight. Puffy cheeks due to swollen salivary glands. Hair loss, dry hair or skin, or excessive facial or body hair.

6. PHYSIOLOGICAL CHANGES: Develops unusual sleep patterns and a sensitivity to cold, feels faint or tired, and menstrual cycles stop or become irregular.

7. EXCESSIVELY RESTRICTING FOODS: Considers certain foods or food groups completely off-limits. Preoccupied with dieting, fat grams, or calories. Equates eating with self-control. Lack of interest in food.

8. EXCESSIVE FEAR: Avoids certain foods for fear of choking or purging. This applies to those suffering from severe restrictive food intake disorder.

9. OVERCONSUMPTION OF FOOD: Frequently consumes very large amounts of food and seems out of control during these binge-eating episodes. Shows a pattern of eating when not hungry and eats to the point of discomfort.

10. PURGING: May compensate for eating through vomiting, laxative or diuretic abuse, or other substances. Leaves the table soon after the meal to purge.

11. SECRETIVE EATING: Large amounts of food disappear over short periods of time. The presence of wrappers or containers might indicate the secret consumption of large quantities of food.

12. EATING RITUALS: Obsessively cut food into small pieces or arrange food to create the appearance of eating while little or no food is consumed.

13. ISOLATION: Withdraws from usual friends and activities. Isolates and gets moody, especially after eating. May make continual excuses about not being able to eat with others.

If you see signs and symptoms of an eating disorder, take them seriously. NEDA is a great resource for help and support in your area. Their helpline number is 800-931-2237, and their website can be found at https://www.nationaleatingdisorders.org/help-support/contact-helpline. A good starting point is to make an appointment with your family doctor.

Physical Activity

Physical activity will increase your child's grade point average. According to scientific research by the California College of San Diego, exercise improves memory and information-processing functions. If practiced on a regular basis, it can boost GPAs. Here's how it works. When kids exercise, carbohydrates are broken down into glucose, which is sugar. Glucose is literally food for the brain. Regular exercise creates glucose storage in two parts of the brain critical for memory and learning—the hippocampus and the neocortex. Cardiovascular exercise is particularly effective for increasing glycogen stores and enlarging the brain. In essence, exercise feeds the brain and makes it larger and smarter.

Regular exercise not only boosts memory and learning but also decreases the risk of mental and physical illness in children. It reduces depression and anxiety by producing endorphins, brain chemicals responsible for improving mood. Consistent exercise also helps kids control weight, which prevents diabetes and heart disease. Overall, kids who exercise regularly have higher self-esteem, are more confident, and get better sleep.

Adults need about 150 minutes of exercise per week. The CDC reports that only 23 percent of adults follow this recommendation. Teens need about one hour of physical activity almost every day. Unfortunately, only three in ten teens meet these guidelines, and the ones who don't have been compared to sixty-year-olds regarding exercise habits. We must get our kids moving! It doesn't have to be so intense that it turns them off. You want to find something they like that keeps them moving almost daily. Here are some tips for encouraging healthy exercise for your child:

- **Start with small changes.** For those who are not in the habit of exercising, here is what I know. It is often more the *thought* of doing it that demotivates a person than doing the exercise. For example, your child gets home from school and wants to play video games. You suggest he/she exercise, and they bristle. Negotiate with them. They can control how long and intensely they exercise. It may be only ten minutes. They are likely to be more motivated because they know it won't take long. What usually happens is they forget about the time because it feels good. The fact that they know they are in control is liberating. Consistency, six to seven days every week, even if only ten minutes, is most important for developing and sustaining a routine.

- **It is more effective to make it fun than intense.** It is easy to associate exercise with work or strain on the body. If you can find activities involving fun movements, kids are more likely to engage. For example, some kids don't necessarily like to "exercise" but enjoy being outdoors. Canoeing, hiking, nature walks, or swimming may be options.

- **Focus on health, not weight loss.** Exercising for weight loss is okay. However, it can also lead to negative associations. Educate your child on the mental and physical health benefits of exercise to change from a negative to a positive mindset. Physically active people have bigger brains, live longer lives, and are generally happier.

- **Find the right activity.** Experiment. Try something new each week. Talk to your child and find out what they like. Remember, if it is fun, it doesn't feel like work!

- **Find activities you can do together.** It does not matter how old your kids are. There are always things to do together that are fun, physically healthy, and a great way to connect with each other. Take turns as a family choosing different activities.

Within the past few years, my son and I have discovered disc golf, which is a fun way to connect and keeps us moving.

- **Model good habits for your child.** My fondest childhood memories are of running with my father. I watched him quit smoking at forty years old and take up running. He ran daily and got me interested in running races. To this day, I exercise regularly and model good physical health habits for my kids.

Chapter 8 Assignment:

Review each section. Assess what is currently working well and what you need to work on. Based on the suggestions provided, negotiate a plan that works best for your child and family. Be sure to formalize it by writing it out as an ongoing reference point. Determine a regular time to review weekly, monthly, or quarterly, and modify the plan as necessary.

CHAPTER 9:

Step 6—Infuse Emotional Intelligence Skills

THERE HAS LONG been a debate in the fields of business and education about what factors contribute more to success in school, at work, and in life. It has been coined the "IQ vs. EQ" debate. IQ is short for intelligence quotient, while EQ stands for emotional intelligence.

You or your child may have taken an IQ test to assess intelligence levels at some point. Here's what an IQ test measures:

- **Visual and spatial processing:** your ability to mentally manipulate 3D objects.
- **Knowledge of the world:** general knowledge about pop culture and history.
- **Fluid reasoning:** analysis of patterns and puzzles.
- **Working memory and short-term memory:** memory recall.
- **Quantitative reasoning:** the application of basic mathematics skills to the analysis and interpretation of real-world quantitative information.

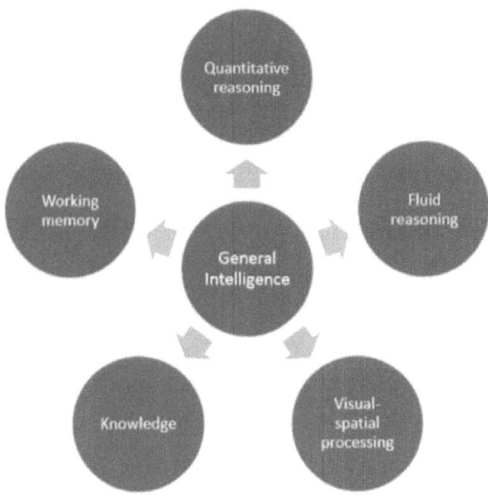

The basis behind traditional IQ tests is to measure our genetic potential for learning and is believed, for the most part, to be unchangeable throughout our lifetime. The presumption is that we are all born with a level of intelligence that remains the same throughout our life span and dictates our success.

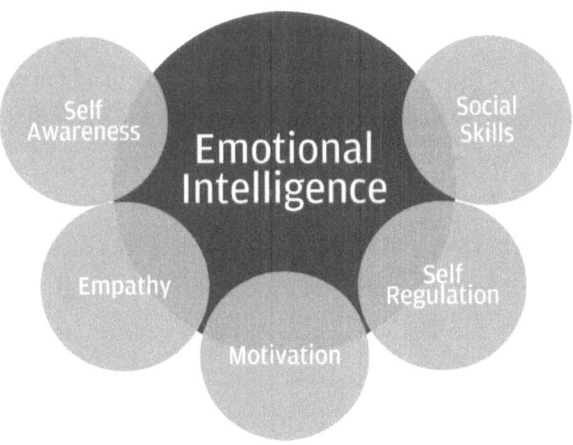

Here's an example of what an EQ test measures:
- **Self-awareness:** how aware we are of our feelings at any given moment.

- **Self-regulation and self-management:** how well we express and manage our emotions.
- **Social skills:** how well we relate to others.
- **Empathy:** how well we understand the experience of others.
- **Motivation:** personal drive to improve and achieve.

The concept of emotional intelligence has been around for a very long time. Dr. Daniel Goleman, whom I referred to in chapter six, has done groundbreaking research demonstrating how crucial these skills are for success in the workplace. In his research, he sought to discover characteristics that set star performers apart from others. And it wasn't the people with the highest IQs. Evidence shows that IQ only contributes 10 to 20 percent to an individual's success in the workplace. Leaders and star performers are individuals with high degrees of emotional intelligence.

Emotional intelligence equates to possessing highly developed social skills. It is important to note, however, that although IQ may only contribute 10 to 20 percent to an individual's success in the workplace, we can't assume that EQ is the other 80 to 90 percent. Goleman points out that some of his past studies have been misinterpreted to make that very assumption. There simply hasn't been enough research to quantify with that degree of accuracy what percentage emotional intelligence plays in success. Other social factors must be taken into consideration. That said, companies are now aware of how critical it is to have employees with highly developed social/emotional intelligence skills. Most of them use aspects of emotional intelligence in their recruiting, promotion, and leadership development processes.

The same holds true in education. It is now common knowledge that kids with higher degrees of emotional intelligence not only get better grades but also stay in school longer. Would you be surprised to learn that positivity predicts college students' first-year GPAs better than SAT scores? Hard to believe, isn't it? It's true. The three strongest predictors of making it through college to graduation are being socially responsible, learning to manage impulses, and having empathy for others. These are all characteristics of an emotionally intelligent student. Steven Stein and colleagues, in their book, *The Student EQ Edge: Emotional Intelligence and Your Academic and Personal Success*, present studies that highlight the correlation between emotional intelligence, grade point averages, and school success.

More than two decades ago, the Collaborative for Academic, Social, and Emotional Learning (CASEL) defined the term, social and emotional learning (SEL). SEL is about integrating emotional intelligence skills into school systems. As published in *Child Development*, CASEL produced a series of cutting-edge results in 2017 from a meta-analysis they conducted on 213 social and emotional learning programs in schools. The study found that approximately 50 percent of kids enrolled in SEL programs had better achievement scores, and almost 40 percent showed improved grade point averages. These programs were also linked to lowered suspension rates, increased school attendance, and reduced disciplinary problems. Based on eight studies that measured academic performance, research revealed that students exposed to emotional intelligence programs were an average of thirteen percentile points higher than their non-SEL peers. Conduct problems, emotional distress, and drug use were all significantly lower for students exposed to SEL programs.

The evidence is overwhelming. Emotional intelligence is extremely important for success in school, work, and life. Unlike traditional measures of IQ, EQ doesn't remain the same over our life span. It is heavily impacted by our environment and our interaction with others. There is much we can do as parents, teachers, coaches, and mentors to help our children raise their EQs!

The Neuro of Emotional Intelligence

Before I explain the skill sets involved in emotional intelligence, I want to help you understand EQ on a deeper level. Below is the figure I presented in chapter six.

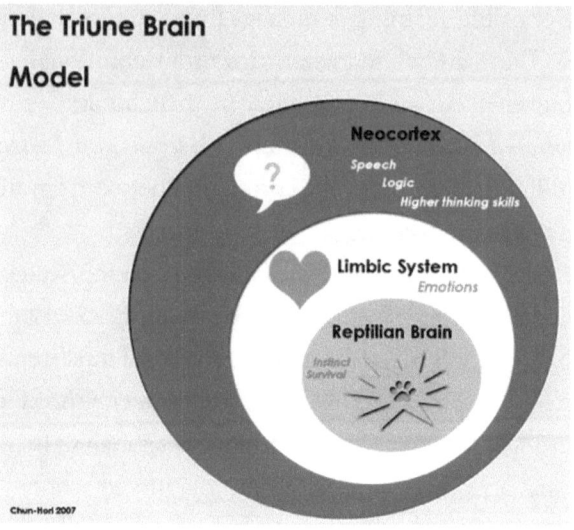

The brain grows and develops from the bottom up, beginning with the most primitive, instinctual reptilian brain to the mid-brain, which is the limbic system. The limbic system is responsible for assigning and managing emotions based on how we experience the environment around us. The outer part of the brain, the neocortex, is responsible for higher-order thinking skills. A pathway of electrical signals begins in the lower brain and travels up through the limbic system to the outer brain. When our kids are sorting out feelings and deciding how to act on them, there is a complex interplay between the emotional and rational parts of the brain. Think of the emotional part of the brain as the feeling part and the rational part of the brain as the thinking part. Kids with high emotional intelligence skills can sort out thoughts and feelings and make good decisions in the moment. Imagine your teen in a group of friends at a party, feeling happy and excited to be with each other, when one of their peers asks them to do something risky, like jump off the roof of the garage into a pool in the backyard. Your child is caught up in the heat of the moment and feels intense peer pressure to make the jump. There is a split second of a time when their brain must process the moment and decide.

The more we teach emotional intelligence skills and the more our children practice them, the stronger the neural connections become between the rational and emotional parts of the brain. There is a term in neurobiology called "plasticity." Plasticity is a measure of how our brains adapt to change. This is like lifting weights. The more we lift, the more muscle fiber we develop and the more physically strong we become. The more our kids practice emotional intelligence skills, the more efficiently the emotional and rational parts of their brains communicate, resulting in better decision-making, such as choosing not to jump off the roof of the garage into the pool.

Neural communication occurs not only through pathways in the brain but also between people. We now know through neuroscience that we have a certain percentage of neurons in our brains that imitate each other, known as mirror neurons. We literally "Bluetooth" with each other. Our neural connection with our kids is important for healthy brain development and very much a part of teaching emotional intelligence. Parents and teens need to sync up more with each other and less with wireless devices. We can teach our kids very powerful lessons through modeling. Think about a high school baseball coach teaching kids the fundamentals of fielding a ground ball and throwing it to first base. He goes into detail about a complex set of movements and body positioning that must take place to be successful.

"Athletic position. Move your feet. Soft hands. Solid base." When it is time for the kids to try, the coach gets frustrated. "Don't you remember what I told you? Move your feet! Soft hands!" The following week, the coach brings in a recent high school graduate who is playing college baseball. He hits balls to him as his players sit on the bench and watch. They observe him as he crouches into an athletic position, feet shoulder-width apart, knees slightly bent, glove to the ground. They see him quickly move his feet to get in front of the ball. The ball is moving fast and bouncing hard as it comes toward him. Moving with the energy of the ball, like a martial artist practicing Tai Chi, he scoops it up and makes a perfect throw to first base with one fluid motion. The kids on the bench go wild. "Did you see that?

OMG, that was cool! He's really smooth." When the kids begin to field ground balls, the coach notices that they perform much better than last week. They learned and internalized fundamental skills by watching and identifying with the older, more experienced player. When our children witness us using skills like managing emotions, socializing, or demonstrating empathy for others, we activate and strengthen their neural networks, which are involved in developing these skills.

Our "Bluetooth" connection with our kids is wonderful. We use it to teach thousands of lessons, from patty-cake and peekaboo, how to use a spoon, potty training, and minding your manners in public. As exciting as it is to know about the power of mirror neurons, it is important to understand that there is a dark side. Have you ever heard a toddler blurt out a swear word? You are surprised to hear such profanity come out of a little person's mouth. You wonder, *Where did they learn that?* When our kids are exposed to environments with negativity, such as extensive yelling and hostility, we are also building these neural networks.

When I work with families, I often must intervene and change the energy in the room. Emotions can become contagious and take over. I'll have a mother and daughter in my office getting into heated arguments. I feel the energy in my body, and for a split second, I am urged to raise my voice along with them. There can be a diminishing point of marginal returns on emotions. I encourage emotional expression to gain mutual understanding, resolve conflicts, and deepen connections.

However, sometimes, when emotions get too high, we get stuck in "limbic lava," and meaningful communication shuts down. If sustained for long periods of time, it can become abusive and damaging. As a therapist, I must sense when this is happening and change the energy. Parents, you can do this too. If your child is upset and having difficulty calming down, finding a way to change the energy is extremely helpful. It might mean taking time out from the conversation and committing to revisit later. Model deep breathing and modulate your tone. A calm presence is much more powerful than words in helping children regulate emotions.

Self-Awareness

Self-awareness is the foundational building block to the other emotional intelligence skills discussed in this book. Self-aware teens can identify feelings in any given moment and act in accordance. When our children cannot correctly identify feelings, they can make mistakes with coping behaviors. And often, teens struggle to separate thoughts from feelings. I have had kids in my office who report feeling "like a loser," "stupid," or "like punching someone in the mouth." These are not feelings but self-judgments and thoughts that can lead to responses that escalate problems. Feelings are emotional states that take place in the body.

Let's go back to my example of the child standing on top of the garage needing to make a split-second decision about jumping into the pool. He comes into my office with stitches in his forehead and bumps and bruises all over his body. I ask him how he felt before he jumped, and he responds, "I felt like I had to jump because some of my buddies already had."

I ask, "How could you tell you were feeling like you had to jump? Where did you experience it in your body?"

He says, "What do you mean? I felt like I had to jump!"

"Let's revisit that moment on top of the garage," I say. "What was happening in your chest? Was your heart beating fast or slow?" He tells me his heart was pounding. "How was your breath? Was it deep and slow, or was it shallow and fast?"

"I was holding my breath," he explains.

"And what was happening in your stomach?"

"It was all jittery and a little bit sick." I give him a list of emotional states to consider—happy, sad, mad, scared, embarrassed, excited, and guilty. "Scared and embarrassed," he explains.

"Okay, so you felt embarrassed and scared."

"Yes," he says. I then help him tease out the thoughts connected to each of these emotional states. Embarrassment led to the thought, *Everyone is going to laugh at me if I don't jump. They're going to talk about me being a wimp on Instagram.* The thought connected to the fear was *I'm not sure if I can make the jump, and I could get hurt.* I work to help him understand that when his brain misinterprets his feelings, he limits his options.

"There is no such thing as feeling like you have to jump," I tell him. "You felt embarrassed and scared, and in the heat of the moment, your brain came up with only one option, so you jumped." This is an example of how kids can make poor choices when they are unaware of the difference between what they think and how they feel.

Know Your Triggers

In addition to being clear about thoughts, feelings, and the difference between the two, another very important aspect of self-awareness is knowing your "triggers." A trigger is an event or situation that can lead to a stress reaction. Triggers are usually caused by something in the surrounding environment or another person's actions. Our children are often unaware of their triggers and need help managing them. Below are some of the most common triggers for high school students, most of which were mentioned previously in chapter four.

- **Academic stress.** Exams and deadlines can trigger anxiety, especially if your child hasn't developed good time management skills.
- **Social media.** Comparing themselves to others and experiencing harassment, humiliation, or rejection on social media can be extremely disturbing for teens.
- **Family problems.** Divorce, separation, marital problems, sibling disputes, and financial struggles all contribute to anxiety, which can make it hard to focus on school.
- **World events.** Kids have access to world news twenty-four

seven and can become easily overwhelmed by hearing about school shootings, acts of terrorism, or natural disasters.

- **Traumatic events.** Death of family members, car accidents, sickness, and enduring emotional or physical abuse is very stressful for kids.
- **Significant life changes.** Moving, starting at a new school, divorce, separation, and the blending of families can be significant sources of stress.
- **Peer pressure.** By nature, teens have an intense need to fit in with peers. Negative peer pressure can result in poor choices around substance use, sexual behaviors, and how they treat others—for example, bullying behaviors.
- **Parental pressure.** As parents, if we constantly put pressure on our kids to perform in every aspect of life, we can inadvertently set them up for failure.

Self-Defeating Behaviors

As we become more self-aware, we gain insight into our thoughts, feelings, and sources of stress, as well as our default coping patterns. A default pattern of behavior is something we have learned to do to cope with the stress that becomes problematic. Doctor Phil asks his clients, "How's that working for you?" Jack's case study, as mentioned in chapter 4, exemplifies how kids can get stuck in self-defeating patterns of behavior due to stress. He struggled greatly, not only with his parent's divorce but also with their ongoing co-parenting disagreements. He became angry and pessimistic and began getting into physical altercations. He got so far behind in school that he gave up trying. As a member of the hockey team, he violated substance abuse policies, knowing that it could jeopardize his playing status. When he felt safe enough to identify and express his true feelings, he became aware of how he had been coping by engaging in self-defeating behaviors. Here are some common self-defeating behaviors teens engage in. Look at the list below and see if any of the behaviors pertain to your child:

- Smoking and vaping
- Skipping classes at school
- Not asking for help
- Avoiding self-care
- Substance abuse
- Hanging out with kids who get in trouble
- Giving up
- Not studying
- Procrastinating
- Yelling and screaming
- Not listening
- Bullying
- Social media and video game addiction
- Isolating
- Under-eating or overeating
- Self-injurious behaviors

Now that you know what self-defeating behavior is, you may want to think of some of your default patterns. We all have them. One of mine, for example, is to ignore self-care when I get involved in a big project. My faulty thinking is *I don't have time for anything else*. These thoughts can backfire on me as I get tired and my creativity and productivity go down. A good way to broach this subject with your child is to explain that everyone has self-defeating behavior patterns, including you. You could start the discussion by disclosing one of yours. The more you normalize discussions about thoughts, feelings, sources of stress, and self-defeating behaviors, the more open your child will be to talking about theirs.

Values

Knowing your values is a cornerstone of self-awareness. One of my colleagues shared a story about an experience she had with her son. He had come home after an evening at a teen coffee house. He was elated! He and his friend had found a large bag of silver dollars under a tree in the parking lot. They split the coins, and her son was convinced that he could sell the silver dollars and get enough money to buy a new guitar. My colleague reported that when she looked at the coins, some of them were in cases, indicating they had been cared for. "Honey, this is somebody's collection," she told her son. "I'm not going to tell you what to do here, but I am going to ask you to think about what the right thing to do is." After thinking about it overnight, he decided to call the police and turn the coins in. She praised him profusely for "doing the right thing." By giving him the space to examine his values and praising him for making a good decision, his mom reinforced values of honesty, integrity, and concern for others.

It is important to look for teachable moments to instill values. When values are instilled early on, they become guiding principles that act as an inner compass, directing us through life. Our kids internalize rules for living that become almost an unconscious way of being. They are grounded in who they are and where they are going in life. In an age where our iGen kids are vulnerable to being negatively influenced by thousands of messages that bombard them every day from the internet, cell phones, and other forms of wireless technology, it is imperative that we are vigilant about teaching and instilling core values.

Strengths and Weaknesses

While values are learned and can be reinforced, we are all born with an inherent and unique set of personality traits. It is helpful to reflect on and determine areas of strength and areas of weaknesses. In chapter two, I disclosed my struggles, not only with ADHD but also with a nonverbal learning disability, which results in visual and spatial deficits. In other words, I have difficulties reading maps, getting from point A to point B, and organizing my physical space. I am aware that this is a major weakness for me. I have also learned that while I struggle to operate in the physical world, I am particularly adept at navigating what is unseen. For example, when I work with couples, I intuitively know how to "map out" the psychological landscape and assist them in moving from point A to point B in their relationship. This is a major strength for me. In coming to a point where I have identified and accepted my strengths and weaknesses, I can direct my energy where it needs to be. I know when to ask for help and what kind of support I need. What is your greatest strength? What is your weakness? Can you talk about them without embarrassment or judgment?

To teach your child to be self-aware, you must first develop your own sense of self-awareness. How often do you identify and talk about feelings in your daily routine with your child? Are you okay with anger? Are you okay with your child's anger? How tuned in are you to your physical states when feeling emotions? Do you know what your personal triggers are? How aware are you of your own self-defeating and default patterns of behavior? What are your values? What are your strengths and weaknesses? Look at the tips below. It may be useful for you to read through them and apply them to yourself before you begin working with your child.

Tips for Teaching Your Child Self-Awareness

- **Teach and instill feelings and feelings language.** There is no such thing as feeling "like" something. Feelings are generally described with one word: happy, mad, sad, relieved, etc. You can go on the internet and find examples of feeling charts that provide helpful pictures and descriptions of a variety of emotions.

- **Accept your feelings without judgment.** Feelings are neither bad nor good. They are messages that compel us to act and influence our decision-making. For example, say you become aware that you are angry with your child for leaving a mess in the kitchen. You're not a bad parent for getting angry. Your anger signals that you must do something, such as asking them to clean up and respect the rules of the house.

- **Feelings are emotional states that occur in the body.** Revisit an intensely emotional experience your child had. Explore and identify the sensations involved in their body. Ask guiding questions. "Where did you feel it in your body? Was your heart beating fast or slow? What was your breathing like? Were your palms sweating? Was your throat tight? How did your stomach feel?" Guided questions help your child understand how physical sensations are connected to emotional states.

- **Know your triggers.** Share the information above to teach your child what a trigger is. Review the examples and have your child identify the triggers that fit them. Work with them to explore triggers that are unique to their experience.

- **Identify your self-defeating behaviors.** Share the information above on self-defeating behaviors with your child. Review the list to see if any of these are a fit. Work to identify any others that may not be mentioned above. Be open to sharing some of your own self-defeating behaviors to normalize this process for your child.

- **Identify your values.** A great way to identify values is through affiliation with structured organizations such as a church, Boy and Girl Scouts, martial arts, sports, and meditation centers. Another powerful way to teach values is by presenting ethical dilemmas. "What would you do if . . ." You can make a game of it or use it as a discussion topic over dinner. Have each family member take turns presenting an ethical dilemma and share beliefs.

- **Acknowledge and accept your strengths and weaknesses.** Help your child explore and identify their strengths and weaknesses. It is important to help them understand that we all have both. Talk to them about yours to increase their comfort level when identifying their own.

Self-Management

Self-management builds based on self-awareness and is the ability to control our emotions—so they don't control us. Think of it this way. Self-awareness is what *is,* and self-management is what we *do* about what is. Again, I will return to the story of the young man who followed his impulse to jump off the garage roof. What would it have been like if he had breathed and exhaled slowly in that short window of time before jumping? Remember our discussion about the "neuro" of emotional intelligence? Imagine him taking a breath, setting off a chain reaction of signals—from the lower brain, through the limbic system, to the outer brain—and deciding to walk away. It can happen that fast. Taking a breath in a crucial moment is one example of using self-management skills.

Emotional Regulation

Because our children's brains are not fully developed as teens, they need our support to learn how to regulate emotions. Emotions are like ocean waves. Some are calm and gentle, and some are fierce and crashing. Our task is to teach our teens to ride the waves without being pulled under. You have been doing this all along. Think back to when your child was a toddler. I'm sure you can remember a temper tantrum or two. Let's say you told your child, "No!" In response, they had an intense emotional experience. Maybe she threw herself on the floor and screamed at the top of her lungs. Maybe he stomped around and broke his toys. As a parent, you likely had several strategies up your sleeve to help your child calm down. Perhaps you diverted their attention by giving them a snack or some reassurance that everything was going to be okay. Some parents ignore their child's tantrums or provide time-outs so as not to reinforce the behavior. Despite your attempts to communicate by use of language—"What's wrong? Why don't you listen! Calm down!"—you intuitively know that your toddler lacks the sophistication and skills to communicate their needs. As they move through childhood to adolescence and improve language skills, it is easy to get lulled into thinking that they have the capacity to articulate what they need. We become surprised as they seem to revisit the "terrible twos." We get tricked into believing that because they look mature, they are mature. We start to believe they don't need us to help them with emotional regulation when, in fact, they need us more.

I had a mom in my office a few years ago. She struggled immensely with her daughter, Amy, who had recently transitioned from a small private middle school to a large public high school. When she arrived, she didn't know anyone and was stressed out about making friends and being accepted. Amy began isolating herself in her room and snapping at her mom when asked about her day. Her mother said she would "mope" around the house and bring everyone "down." She frequently locked herself in the bathroom and spent hours on her cell phone talking to friends from her old school. In one of our sessions with her mother, Amy became intensely emotional, stormed out, and slammed the door. As she was leaving, I told her it was okay to take a break, but we would like her to return.

After several minutes, Amy returned to my office and slumped down into a chair. I thanked her for coming back and asked her how she was feeling. She immediately started yelling at me. "How would you feel if your mom was ragging on you all the time?"

Mom jumped in and yelled at her. "Be respectful!"

I turned to Mom and asked her to hold that thought while I worked to help Amy express her true feelings. I could feel the intensity in the room. I asked her to take a long, deep breath with me. She rolled her eyes. I said, "Come on, humor me." I demonstrated a breath in through my nose and exhaled slowly through my mouth.

She said, "Why doesn't my mom have to do it?"

I replied, "Good point. Mom, how would you like to take a crack at this with us?" We took one breath together. I asked them to do it again. "One more time, just for fun," I said. After three deep breaths, I noticed a shift in energy. I asked her again how she was feeling and gave her some options from a feeling chart.

"Really, really angry," she said.

"Here is what I know about anger," I explained. "Anger is like a shield, and there is usually another feeling behind it." She began to sob in the chair. I gave her a few minutes and validated that it was not only okay to cry but also good for her.

Amy expressed hurt and sadness for having to leave her school and not being able to see her friends. I helped her make a connection between her feelings of hurt and sadness and the anger coming out. I turned to Mom and asked her if she was aware of how much Amy was hurting. Mom had tears in her eyes. "No, I wasn't. I just thought she was mad and being selfish and disrespectful. I had no idea she was in this much pain." As Amy wept, her mother apologized for not understanding how stressed out she was over the new school transition. In future sessions, when Amy got upset, Mom became calmer and more nurturing rather than getting defensive and yelling. She became a better listener, learned to validate her daughter's feelings, and was much more open to respecting her point of view. Amy learned to identify and process feelings rather than acting out. As she became more adept at regulating her emotions in sessions, her mother was happy to report that Amy had been using these newfound skills at home and school. Consider the tips below to help your teen regulate emotions.

- **Give them space.** When our kids are upset—and in their lower brains, reptilian fight-or-flight—we are only adding fuel to the fire if we keep pushing them. Take a break and let them know you will revisit the topic later.
- **Understand that anger could mask other emotions.** Don't always take anger at face value. Most often, when kids present

as angry, there is a more important underlying emotion they are struggling with.

- **Respect differing perspectives.** Sometimes, we need to consider our children's viewpoints (for example, school life). Parents often forget how important social life is to kids and only see through the lens of grades or performance. Remember, when socially connected, kids perform better in school and life.

- **Bite your tongue.** Sometimes we must take a breath and hold in our thoughts. When you feel yourself getting worked up—heavy breathing, elevated heart rate, sweaty palms, and you are ready to blow, or you see your child is ready to blow—bite your tongue and wait for things to cool down.

- **Be calm.** Remember, feelings are contagious. Don't get pulled in. You may have to take a few deep breaths to center yourself before approaching your child. We have an energetic connection with our kids. The best way to help them regulate emotions is to approach with a calm presence. A calm presence is much more effective than words when our kids struggle emotionally.

- **Validate feelings.** As I mentioned earlier, feelings aren't good or bad. Let your child know that whatever they are feeling is okay. When they calm down, help them identify feelings. If they struggle with this, feelings charts are very helpful.

- **Be a role model.** The better we regulate our emotions, the better our children will be able to do so. Talk about feelings with them and share techniques you use to regulate emotions and cope with stress. For example, deep breathing, meditation, physical activity, reading, and leisure activities.

- **Consider therapy.** If your child struggles with regulating emotions despite your best efforts, consider seeing a therapist for help. There may be a deep underlying issue that needs to be addressed professionally.

Impulse Control

Think back to your first few months away from home, on a college campus, with many high-energy kids your age. So much newfound freedom and so many choices to make! The *Annual Review of Clinical Psychology* is a widely established clinical journal that publishes research articles. In January 2019, it was reported that children with high self-control perform better academically. A very important aspect of self-control is the capacity to manage impulses. Impulse control is the ability to delay gratification and stay focused on long-term goals, such as getting good grades, attending college, and excelling in sports, music, theatre, or vocational apprenticeships. According to the review, nearly all students struggle with conflicts between long-term goals and short-term goals that they find more alluring and gratifying in the moment. Lack of impulse control can lead to self-defeating behaviors that compromise success in achieving long-term goals. I interviewed about fifty college students who corroborated this evidence. As you can probably guess, cell phones, social media, and video games were major distractors to focusing on schoolwork. Lack of impulse control can lead to other self-defeating behaviors, such as skipping classes, substance abuse, bullying, and procrastination. Parents, now is the time to work with your child on learning to manage impulses and avoid self-defeating behaviors. Look at the tips below:

- **Get clear on the big picture.** The more grounded your child is in "big picture" goals, the more capacity they will have to manage impulses and avoid self-defeating behaviors. Talk about big-picture goals (for example, GPAs, areas of study, and career aspirations). Let them know how excited you are for them. Have a "SWOT" discussion in which you identify strengths, weaknesses, opportunities, and threats. What is your greatest strength? What is a work area for you? What are your opportunities? What are possible threats to your big-picture goals moving forward? Write these down in a journal for future reference.

- **Establish clear expectations and boundaries.** Establish clear expectations and boundaries around school attendance, study time, substance use, screen time, time with friends, and curfews. Stress that your expectations are not about controlling; rather, it's about success in life. Clear expectations and boundaries will raise your child's level of awareness, resulting in better impulse control and fewer self-defeating behaviors.

- **Self-monitoring.** When your child engages in self-defeating behavior, stay calm and help them think through the incident. Ask them some questions. Where were you? What was happening? Can you remember how you were feeling? What were you thinking? Work to help them identify a choice they can use next time that will result in a better outcome.

- **Teach your teen to delay gratification.** Let them know they can go out with friends when they finish their homework. Talk to them about screen time. Encourage them to stay away from phones and social media while doing schoolwork. Set aside time for them to enjoy electronics as a reward. Have them turn off their cell phones before bed or move them into a different room.

- **Encourage your child to breathe.** Teen years are full of excitement and emotion, creating challenges with impulse control. Taking time to breathe calms the brain down, resulting in higher levels of self-awareness and better decision-making. Coach your child to remember to breathe before making decisions that could result in self-defeating behavior.

Social Skills

To this point, I have been discussing emotional intelligence within the context of self-awareness—being aware of emotions in any given moment—and self-management—how we manage our emotions. Following his book on emotional intelligence in 1995, Dr. Goleman wrote another book in 2006, *Social Intelligence: The New Science of Human Relationships*, which introduces two important areas when developing social skills: *social awareness* and *social facility*. You can think about these in the same way I discussed self-awareness and self-management above. Social awareness is your child's ability to sense how others think and feel. Social facility is your child's ability to interact most effectively based on this knowledge. Social awareness is what *is*, and social facility is what we *do* about what is.

In his book, Dr. Goleman celebrates the emergence of "social neuroscience" and its contributions to understanding how we relate and interact with each other as human beings. As previously discussed, we now know about mirror neurons. Goleman describes them as an internal "Wi-Fi" system. Our brains synchronize with each other on a primal level, allowing us to make split-second decisions on how to interact socially. He underscores the importance of brain plasticity. By practicing social skills, we build and strengthen brain pathways responsible for successful execution. Socially intelligent teens can connect well with others and have their needs met in social situations.

Social Awareness

At the core of social awareness is the ability to sense how others think and feel. We do this by reading and interpreting both verbal and nonverbal cues. Verbal cues are generally communicated through spoken language. Nonverbal cues involve body posture, body movement, facial expressions, voice tones, and pace of speech. As we become aware of these cues, we need to put them in context with our social setting. What may be appropriate at a high school pep fest would not be appropriate in the library.

I learned about the importance of social awareness in my first job out of high school, working as a waiter in a busy restaurant. Being socially aware could mean the difference between walking home with a nice wad of cash in your pocket or being frustrated by how low your tips were. As I approached my tables, I learned to read facial expressions and body language quickly and adapt to the needs of my customers. A group of businessmen coming in for lunch, dressed in suits, with serious facial expressions, monotone voices, and rigid body postures, are not concerned about small talk with me. They are focused on each other, talking about work, and in a hurry to eat lunch and return to the office. They want quick, efficient service and nothing else. Two women who came from the bar with martinis in their hands, chatting and laughing, with relaxed body postures, may smile warmly and begin to engage me in conversation. I would quickly assess that they are not in a hurry and want to enjoy themselves. Part of their experience is to chat and share some humor with me. I would take time out to smile, laugh, and joke with them. At the table next to them might have been a mom and dad, with an infant in a car seat and a toddler who is a bundle of energy. I would observe Mom's red face and watch as Dad reached over the table, trying to get his kid to sit still. It would appear they had been out shopping all day and needed to feed their kids. I would sense they were both tired and worried about their kids making a scene in the restaurant. I would bring crayons and crackers to the table for the kids, and Mom would thank me profusely. They would vent to me about their busy day, and I would tell them they have nothing to worry about. "I understand. I was a kid once myself."

Social Facility

Social facility is the action phase of social awareness. We have received and interpreted the information and are now responding. If we receive information verbally and nonverbally, it makes sense that our response is both verbal and nonverbal. Some important components of social facility are attending to the energy, self-presentation, anticipating needs, active listening, demonstrating concern, and shaping the outcome.

Below are examples of how I used these skills to interact with my customers.

- **Attending to the energy.** In the restaurant, as I approached a table of businessmen, I matched their energy by being business-like, serious, and efficient. As I approached a table with the women drinking martinis, I used humor, a more relaxed pace, and small talk.

- **Self-presentation.** With businessmen, I presented myself as a confident, no-nonsense professional. I shared my casual, personable side with a chatty table.

- **Anticipating needs**. With young families, I quickly assessed and anticipated if a diversion was needed to avoid a meltdown. I would bring crackers and coloring crayons to the table.

- **Active listening.** With businessmen, I would demonstrate active listening by repeating their orders word for word to make sure I got it right. If I was really busy—with ten other tables in various dining stages—and a chatty table came into my section, I would put all my anxious thoughts to the side—*Check to table six, milk with meal to table one, I'm tired, I can't wait to get off of my shift, my feet are killing me*—and direct my attention to connecting, listening, and focusing on them one-hundred-percent. I'd listen to stories about their family trip to Mexico and the funny memories of their fishing trip.

- **Demonstrating concern.** I would notice if a young family, with high-energy kids, was flustered. I would put a caring expression on my face and speak softly, assuring them that they didn't have to worry about their kids making a scene.

- **Shaping the outcome.** In each scenario, my goals were the same. I wanted my patrons to have a good time, and I wanted to get a good tip. I had to be socially aware and adjust my responses to optimize the outcome for all of us.

As baby boomers and Gen X parents, we grew up in a very different environment from our kids. Think back to the old neighborhoods. We got up every day and played all kinds of sports and games with each other: kick the can, capture the flag, pom-pom poll away, football, baseball, and the like. We had opportunities every day, all day, to learn and practice social skills, and it happened naturally; we didn't even realize that we were learning anything—we were just having fun. Think about all the arguments you had as kids playing games. We would often get into such heated disagreements that the game would stop, and we would have to negotiate, make compromises, and change rules for the benefit of the group. We also had to tend to each other's emotions, like sticking up for someone who was feeling hurt or being taken advantage of. Sometimes, physical boundaries would be violated, and we would have to make rules about being respectful. We were "synchronized" with each other. At home, we spent much more time with our parents, observing them interact at the grocery store, in church, and with strangers. We learned about humor, sarcasm, and the subtleties of implicit and explicit social communication.

Our internet-generation kids, despite all their privileges, are experiencing a serious deprivation of the basic human contact critical for healthy social and emotional development. In his book, *Social Intelligence, The Science of Human Relationships*, Dr. Goleman reported findings from a 2004 survey of 4,830 people on the impact of television and internet use in the United States. They concluded that for every hour on the internet, face-to-face contact with friends, coworkers, and family fell by twenty-four minutes. Let's put this into perspective. In 2004, it was estimated that the average person in America spent three hours and thirty-nine minutes per day watching television or on the internet. In chapter six, I referred to information from the Pew Research Center indicating that cell phone ownership crossed the 50 percent threshold late in 2012, right when teen depression and suicide began to rise. By 2015, 73 percent of teens had access to smartphones. It was estimated that our internet-generation kids spend a minimum of six hours per day on some electronic device. And to throw gas on the fire, a recent article in *New York Times* cited statistics indicating that this number doubled because of the isolation from the pandemic. Imagine how this translates to lost opportunities to develop social and emotional intelligence! Below is a list of seven skills that I believe are particularly important to focus on as you move forward with your child.

- **Active listening.** This is the art of conversation. Active listeners refrain from interrupting, waiting their turn to speak. They maintain eye contact and use body language to communicate interest. In conversation, an active listener asks questions to gain clarity and paraphrases or repeats information to ensure mutual understanding.

- **Attunement.** Attunement is being fully present for another person. It is the ability to put all thoughts about yourself aside and pay attention completely. You "tune in" to body language, facial expressions, and voice tones. Your verbal and nonverbal responses indicate genuine care and concern. Kids can immediately sense when a parent or caregiver is distracted or disingenuous.

- **Boundaries.** Personal boundaries are guidelines, rules, or limits that a person creates to identify reasonable, safe, and permissible ways for others to behave toward them. It is imperative that kids learn how to set physical and psychological boundaries. Examples of physical boundaries are physical space: how close you can sit or stand next to them; touch: how, when, and where you can touch them; and personal space: room, house, yard, and belongings. Examples of psychological boundaries are personal feelings, beliefs, and values. *My feelings, beliefs, and values are okay. I get to decide where and with whom to share them.*

- **Assertiveness.** An assertive student asks for what they want and need respectfully and openly. They use "I" statements; "When you don't post my grade after I finish an assignment, I feel anxious because I lose track of how I am doing in class. If you cannot post grades immediately, is there another way we could communicate so I know where I stand?"

- **Refusal skills.** Refusal skills build on assertiveness and are crucial for kids to practice to avoid self-defeating behaviors, such as smoking, substance abuse, skipping school, and hanging out with kids who get in trouble. Saying no sounds easy; however, it can result in a tremendous amount of peer pressure. The more kids practice saying no, the more comfortable they become over time.

- **Conflict resolution.** An important aspect of growing up is learning how to address conflicts. Your child needs to communicate their side of the story clearly without yelling and be open to listening to the other's point of view. Once this has been established, both parties negotiate to explore options to resolve the conflict. The end goal is to reach a compromise that works for both parties.

- **Social responsibility.** In order to function productively in the world, we need to understand that we are part of something bigger than ourselves. Our actions, good or bad, have a ripple effect that touches families, friends, and the broader community.

Empathy

I learned about empathy from my parents early in life. We used to get calls from bill collectors looking for payments on utilities. I answered the phone one day, and a person from the gas company asked if my parents were available. I responded with a "no," and he began to talk very sternly with me. "Tell your parents that if they don't pay the gas bill, we'll shut it off!" I remember talking to my parents about it and being very concerned. I could see the stress on their faces as I relayed the message from the "angry man" on the phone.

As much as we struggled financially, my parents always held firm to their values of service to others. They were frequently involved in projects that helped people in need. One day, I remember confronting them after I learned they gave money to a woman who was in danger of losing her apartment. I was mad. "Why are you giving someone three hundred dollars when we can't pay the gas bill?"

My father looked at me and said, "Because she needs it more than we do." He explained that the woman had young children who needed food and a place to live. If they got evicted, they could be separated from each other. These were not uncommon experiences in my family. My parents had enormous empathy and compassion for people. My mother, in her early forties, after raising a family of nine children, started a nonprofit agency with a mission to help families "overcome barriers, believe in themselves, and soar to new heights." She started by putting a large basket out in church, encouraging people to contribute food items to help those less fortunate. Forty-plus years later, Interfaith Outreach is a multimillion-dollar nonprofit organization that provides food, clothing, employment assistance, affordable housing, childcare, after-school programs, and a myriad of other social services.

Empathy builds on all other EQ skills discussed thus far. Research shows that students high in empathy are more engaged in classrooms, have better communication skills, and have higher academic achievement. Parents, research aside, if you only get one takeaway from this book (and I hope you get many), empathy is what your child and our world need most! We tend to think of empathy as the ability to understand the experience of others. While this is generally true, it is more complex. Dr. Goleman defines empathy on three levels. The first level, *cognitive empathy*, refers to our intellectual understanding of how others think. The second level, *emotional empathy*, is how we pick up on the emotions of others. Level three, *empathic concern*, goes beyond thoughts and feelings to action. My parents understood, on an intellectual level, that the woman with the kids was thinking, *I don't know what to do! What's going to happen with my kids?* On an emotional level, they connected with her frustration, fear, and deep love for her children. Based on their understanding of her situation and emotional state, my parents were motivated to act and do something to help.

I am grateful to my parents for modeling and teaching me how to have empathy for others. I observed and had multiple opportunities to practice empathy throughout my childhood. One of my earliest memories was being in our basement with my mother and gang of siblings, making decoupages for a school fundraiser. We laughed and had fun as we applied cutouts onto stained wood pieces, with a fresh lacquer coating to finish our masterpieces. "Mom, are people actually going to buy these? Why are we doing this?"

"The money we raise will help people living in poverty in Biafra," she explained. The following day at school, we watched a documentary reporting the impact of living in poverty in Biafra. Some of it was really hard to watch. The fact that I still remember it today, like yesterday, tells me it was a great way to learn how to have empathy for others.

As you can see by Goleman's layered definition above, learning true empathy is complex. It takes practice and exposure. How, then, are our internet-generation kids, who are so intensely wired into electronics, going to have time to learn and practice empathy? In 2018, Common Sense Media reported that teenagers, ages thirteen to eighteen, spend about nine hours daily online. Children, ages eight to twelve, spend six hours online, while kids, from birth to eight years of age, spend about fifty minutes online. Results from a study by the University of Michigan found a 40 percent decrease in college students' empathy levels over the past thirty years. The sharpest drop occurred in 2000, when digital technology gained popularity among college students. Lack of empathy in teens contributes to teasing, bullying, and cheating on tests. As parents, we must model and teach our kids not only to understand how others think and feel but also to act out of empathic concern. In a 2018 article about social and emotional learning, Michelle Barba identified several competencies for teachers to teach empathy to students. Below are some of her tips for teachers that I have modified:

- **Foster emotional literacy.** An emotionally literate child can read and accurately interpret the emotions of others. Prioritize face-to-face contact and talk about feelings regularly in your household (for example, at dinnertime to enhance your child's abilities).

- **Self-regulation.** Provide opportunities for practices that help manage moods, such as meditation, prayer, yoga, deep breathing, quiet time without electronic devices, soft music, body movement, and physical activity. Self-regulation allows kids to keep emotions in check, giving them more capacity to have empathy for others.

- **Understanding viewpoints of others.** This is the act of emotionally and psychologically stepping into another's shoes. Talk to your kids about taking others' perspectives, like kids with disabilities, kids that get bullied, and kids from low-income families who can't keep up with the latest styles. Consider activities you can engage in as a family to gain a deeper understanding of other perspectives, such as fasting for a day to understand hunger or participating in an overnight sleep-out to learn more about homelessness.

- **Moral imagination.** Books and emotionally charged films can prompt empathetic feelings. For example, *Because of Winn-Dixie* is both a book and a movie about a motherless young girl who moves to a new town and struggles to make friends until she comes across a loveable stray dog. There are hundreds of books and movies that demonstrate empathy through a variety of characters and storylines. Brainstorm a list of these with friends or other parents and set aside time for reading or movie night as a family.

- **Moral identity.** We can help our kids develop moral identities by coming up with mantras, slogans, or family mottos. Growing up, my family motto was to live by the golden rule—treat others the way you would like to be treated. Take some time and have a family discussion about your shared values and come up with your own slogan. Check in periodically to assess how well you are following your motto.

- **Practicing acts of kindness.** Kindness is always good and benefits both parties. Being kind helps children tune in to others' feelings and needs. As we have discussed, tuning into feelings and understanding needs is a big part of learning empathy. The more opportunities to practice acts of kindness our children have, the more "we" and less "me" they become.

- **Collaboration.** Empathy is not a selfish act. It takes place within relationships. When our kids team up with others for a cause they are passionate about, they realize their participation is about being part of something bigger than themselves.

- **Moral courage.** Teach your children about moral courage! The best way to explain this is from a personal story. When I was nine years old, we used to have very competitive spelling and math contests in my classroom. The teacher would start the clock, and we would all begin doing our problems. When we were finished, we would have to stand up. The people who finished last were often chastised. There were two brothers who always finished last. The teacher encouraged us to make demeaning group chants for finishing last. I was very troubled by this. One day, I finally told my father about what was going on in the classroom. He said, "David, that's wrong. You must speak out for these kids." A few weeks later, we were in class, and as we all stood up, finished with our math problems, the teacher led the class in a chant directed at the two brothers. "Dumb bunny, dumb bunny, dumb bunny!" I couldn't take it anymore. I was so afraid of her that I was shaking. I heard my dad's voice telling me that this was wrong. I spoke up and told her to stop. "You can't do that! That's wrong!" The entire class went silent for about a minute. The silence ended with many of my friends verbally agreeing with what I said. I was kicked out of class for having a "frenzy." I cried when I got home because I thought I would get in trouble. Instead, my father praised me for "doing the right thing." My children love this story. Parents, I am sure you have stories about moral courage. Share these stories with your kids to teach them to embrace and practice acts of moral courage.

- **Grow changemakers.** If we provide our kids with opportunities to help others, we not only activate empathy in them but strengthen their identities as changemakers. For example, Feed My Starving Children is a nonprofit agency that uses volunteers to package nutritious meals for children all over the world. They host different groups, from Cub Scouts to church youth groups to kids who choose this activity as part of their birthday party. When they finish, they learn how many meals were made and how many people they served. In this way, it becomes personal and helps them learn firsthand about the impact they can have on the world as changemakers.

Motivation

As I sit here thinking about how parents can impact healthy motivation in children, my thoughts turn to my new puppy. He has been a member of the family for about a week and a half, and we are working on potty training. Up and down the stairs of the deck I go, cheering the dog on and giving him a treat every time he successfully poops outside instead of on the kitchen floor. I allow half an hour of playtime for successful execution. Everything is new, and he is bombarded by stimulation. I frequently hold and pet him so he can calm down and feel safe in his new environment. I cannot wait for the day he goes to the door, cues me that he needs to go out, runs down the stairs of the deck, does his deed, runs back up the stairs of the deck, and jumps into the house on his own. I love my dog, "Lewey," and although I enjoy petting and calming him down, it will be nice when he learns how to self-soothe through play or toys or perhaps our cat "Goldy" when they get used to each other. Oh, what a day that will be! Although I am not suggesting you treat your child like a dog, there is a similar training and behavioral aspect to motivation when kids are young. Think back to potty training your toddler in the good old days. It is like a party every time they go. You reward them with treats or hugs and words of praise when they use the toilet. You applaud them for being gentle with the cat or when they say sorry for hitting their baby brother. You may punish them by giving them a pat on the butt or putting them in their rooms for throwing food on the floor. These are examples of extrinsic motivation. Your child's behavior is motivated by external rewards or punishment.

Parents, you may well know or soon learn that the strictly behavioral approach of offering external rewards or punishment for "good" or "bad" behavior seems to backfire when our kids hit the tween and teen years. We are surprised by some of the decisions our children make or by what we perceive as a lack of motivation. We are caught off guard by these changes and vulnerable to getting tangled in power struggles. No need to feel guilty. You are not alone! Parent-teen power struggles are age-old and just a part of a process that everyone must get through. Our kids need to learn life skills, and we need to change our approach to match their evolving developmental needs. When I ask parents in my practice what they want most for their tweens and teens, it is often related to school, sports, or other performance issues. Research reveals that while rewards and punishment related to performance might be effective in the short-term, they do not lead to long-term motivation or teach the value of hard work and persistence.

It is now known that one of the best predictors of success in school is focusing on and teaching social and emotional skills. Social and emotional skills are synonymous with emotional intelligence skills and a core component of raising a mentally fit and positively motivated child. We reward our kids for getting good grades and keeping rooms clean, but how often do we praise them for how hard they worked regardless of the outcome, take time to talk about feelings and sources of stress, or understand and help others in need? How often do we take time to learn what they are passionate about?

By infusing emotional intelligence skills, motivation shifts from extrinsic/external to intrinsic or internal. Isn't that the end goal of parenting? You want your children to become the conductor of their lives and know that they will not only be able to take care of themselves but make decisions and engage in behavior that creates happiness and fulfillment. As parents, we have not been fully oriented to teaching our kids emotional intelligence skills. Being self- and socially aware and having empathy for others are cornerstones of emotional intelligence and key components of motivation, driving our kids to decide how and where to best focus their energy. Remember, self-awareness—being aware of how we are feeling in any given moment—is *what is* and self-management—how we manage our emotions—is what *we do about what is*. Had my young man on the roof of the garage been able to clearly identify that he was feeling fearful because he was in danger—instead of thinking he had to jump because of intense peer pressure—he may have been motivated to make a better decision. On the same note, socially aware children understand how others around them are thinking and feeling and can respond in the moment to maximize the outcome for everyone.

A socially aware peer may have intervened, advising his buddy not to make the jump because of the danger and helping him save face under peer pressure. He acts out of empathy for his friend, who is feeling great stress and in jeopardy of getting seriously hurt. In the example I shared of my colleague's son who found a bag of rare coins, his mother assisted him in taking some time to examine the values of honesty, integrity, and concern for others, resulting in calling the police and turning the coins in. Children grounded in emotional intelligence skills make better decisions, perform better in school, and are more successful as they leave home and enter the job market. They are better able to discern what type of work they have a passion and propensity for and perform better in job interviews. Here are some tips for instilling internal motivation in your child:

- **Find out what they are good at or something they are passionate about.** As you help your child explore their interests and passions, it may be something they do out of pure enjoyment, with no expectations, or it may put them on a path to something that becomes very important to them. For example, a child who likes using their hands to put things together may have an interesting hobby or later generalize these skills to a profession such as engineering or architecture. Either way, passion creates internal motivation.

- **Focus on effort and persistence over outcomes.** The long-term goal is for our kids to learn skills that last a lifetime. If you focus on praising and rewarding your child only for good performance in school or sports, you may inadvertently be encouraging cheating or taking shortcuts. This is not sustainable and is a disservice to them, as they may find themselves ill-equipped to take on life's challenges in adulthood.

- **Help them learn from mistakes.** I believe there is no such thing as making a mistake. Sure, your child may do something that results in an undesirable outcome. As parents, we can help our kids think through the behavior and consequence to strategize for a better outcome in the future. So, what we think of as a mistake is a stepping stone to a new behavior that leads to success. A child who gets behind in school and makes the "mistake" of not asking for help experiences a natural consequence of getting a bad grade. He or she can be coached to meet with their teacher to get the help they need. Our child's success leads to future internal motivation to ask for help when they need it.

- **Focus more energy on what they are doing right versus wrong.** As parents, we are hardwired to look out for anything we perceive as a threat to our children's health and well-being. It is instinctual, and from an evolutionary standpoint, the ability to detect and mitigate threats was a way to ensure our DNA was passed on through our kids. Often, this carries into how we perceive the decisions they make or how they perform. We focus on what we believe they are doing wrong more than what we believe they are doing right. Think back to your journey of mastery and success. Were you more motivated by focusing on failures, or were you more motivated by focusing on past successes? We are now aware from neuroscience that where and how we focus our energy greatly impacts behavior and outcomes. Children are happier, more confident, and internally motivated to move forward and take charge of their lives by focusing on successes.

- **Give them opportunities to make decisions for themselves.** Think of Maslow's hierarchy of needs as your child's journey to reaching the top of their pyramid toward happiness and fulfillment as adults. It begins with parents providing basic needs and love. Eventually, our children leave and are tasked to fly on their own. Your child's ability to learn to make decisions along the way is empowering. It fuels internal motivation. Make sure to include your tween or teen in the decision-making process by identifying a problem or goal and brainstorming solutions. Help them think through potential consequences, good or bad, to create a plan moving forward. Follow up with them to review the outcome and help them modify the plan as needed.

- **Instill confidence.** It is virtually impossible to be internally motivated if you lack confidence in your ability to succeed. Provide your children opportunities for mastery experiences by setting goals and getting involved in activities that create personal challenges. Sports, academics, chess clubs, learning new languages, and playing instruments are just a few examples. Resist the urge to shield them from failing so they are better able to build resilience and push through setbacks as adults. Getting kids hooked up with mentors is a great way to instill confidence through role modeling and being a trusted voice of encouragement. Acknowledge successes, including their effort and how they overcame obstacles along the way. Anxiety can be a roadblock to internal motivation. Teaching kids reflective practices of slowing down and breathing to sort out thoughts are a great way to reduce anxiety and improve motivation.

Chapter 9: EQ Assignment:

Review this chapter and use your journal to take an inventory of EQ skills you and your family are doing well. Celebrate your accomplishments with each other in a way that suits your family. For example, make a special dinner together or throw a party and play games. Review the chapter again and list growth areas you would like to expand on. Think of growth areas as menu items in a cookbook. Use the tips to create a recipe to develop the EQ skills that you have identified. Let's say you have identified that you want to work on increasing empathy as a family. Your recipe could be as follows: read books and watch movies/moral imagination, develop a family motto/moral identity, and volunteer for a worthy cause/practicing acts of kindness.

CHAPTER 10:

Step 7—Set Realistic Goals and Coach Your Child to Success

GREAT JOB! YOU have learned how the mental fitness model works. Now is the time for the rubber to hit the road. As your child's parent/coach, the best way you can help them achieve goals is by building confidence. Psychologist Albert Bandura, in the 1970s, developed an effective model for instilling confidence, known as "self-efficacy theories." Self-efficacy is a person's belief in their ability to succeed in goal-directed activities. The stronger your child's belief in their ability to cope with stress and succeed in school and life, the more active they become in pursuing goals. And the more active they are, the more successful they will be. Confidence equals activity, and activity equals success. Before you help your child with goal setting, I want to introduce you to Dr. Bandura's sources of self-efficacy.

- **Prior accomplishments.** When we lack confidence and experience self-doubt, it is helpful to reflect on mastery experiences—past performance accomplishments. Think about your child. What are some significant accomplishments they have achieved in the past? Helping your child reflect on past successes is the most dependable source of confidence-building information because it is based on personal experience.

- **Vicarious learning from role models.** One of the best ways to learn is from those who have been successful at the goal you are trying to achieve. Think of vicarious learning as a process of observing, learning, imitating, and acting. Who would be a good role model for your child to learn how from?

- **Verbal persuasion.** When setting goals with your child, be positive and let them know you believe in their ability to succeed. As parents, we know our children's strengths more than anyone else. Speaking out loud and celebrating them is very motivational! Be authentic. Give them honest, constructive, positive feedback. Challenge negative self-talk and replace it with positive affirmations.

- **Arousal/managing emotions.** We all experience anxiety when trying something new. Work with your child on establishing anxiety-reducing practices. Deep breathing and meditation are the number one ways to achieve calm. Yoga is a great stress reducer and has become increasingly popular with teens and young adults. Encourage your child to incorporate physical activity into daily routines. We are now aware, through the field of neuroscience, that a great deal of stress gets stored in our bodies. Physical activity calms the body, which calms the mind. The calmer your child is, the more brainpower they have. When we get anxious, we often develop negative self-talk about our ability to succeed at a goal. In the field of psychology, we call these "distorted" thoughts. Most of us have had them at one time or another when under stress. Coach your child to challenge the reality of negative self-talk and move toward positivity.

- **Imaginary experiences.** Imaginary experiences help your child visualize success. Visualizing success will strengthen the neurological pathways in your child's brain that are responsible for performing well at achieving specific goals. It's like mental practice. Athletes use this for performance improvement in sports. A major league pitcher may take time before the game to imagine every situation he will be up against and picture himself being successful. When it is game time, he will be much better prepared.

You need to be aware of some critical parts of goal setting when working with your child to be successful. Goals need to be specific, measurable, achievable, and time limited. Make sure you write them down. Writing goals down legitimizes your work together. Below is a hypothetical example of a goal-setting framework I commonly use with my clients.

A young woman asks me to be her marathon coach:

Step 1: Identify the goal and write it down.

In my first meeting with this young woman, I ask her, "What is your goal?" She tells me her goal is to complete her first marathon. "Do you want to train to finish, or are you going for a particular time frame?" She explains that her main goal is to finish, but it would be cool if she could make it in under five hours. "Okay, write that down in your journal." Because this is her first marathon, I ask her for a six-month time commitment. She agrees.

Step 2: List the tasks needed to obtain the goal.

Because she is a novice to long-distance running, I tell her where she can buy a good pair of shoes and running apparel appropriate for weather conditions. She needs a water bottle and a stopwatch to keep track of time. I strongly suggest she gets a heart rate monitor. We establish a target heart rate to stay in while she is running to keep her safe, and I give her dietary information about carbohydrates, protein, and fats related to long-distance training. I make sure she knows what complex carbohydrates are. We meet to map out the training schedule. For the first three weeks, she will walk and run fifteen miles per week. From there, mileage and frequency will be added incrementally as she can handle it.

Step 3: Start working on the tasks.

We have a check-in the first week to see if she was able to get the right equipment. I ask her if she has stocked her house with foods that will give her energy. On our third weekly check-in, she tells me that she is getting shin splints. I instruct her to reduce her mileage and ice after she runs.

Step 4: Add to the tasks as needed.

I continue to monitor her progress. She is in week six, running twenty miles per week, pain-free. I add more miles to her weekly regimen and recommend adding more complex carbohydrates to her diet. She works her way up to seventy miles per week in her final month of training. I instruct her to taper down to forty-five or fifty miles a week for the weeks before the big day to give her body a chance to fully recover.

Step 5: Check off the tasks as they are completed.

In our weekly meetings, we check off tasks that have been completed. Each time she finishes a task, we talk about it. We review the steps she took to accomplish the task and how she overcame obstacles or setbacks along the way. I praise her for her hard work.

Step 6: When all the tasks are complete, determine if the goal has been met.

In the final week, she runs twenty miles and takes two days of rest before the marathon. She finishes the run in four hours and fifty-five minutes without injury. We celebrate her accomplishments. She proudly sports her marathon medal around her neck and reports that she can't wait to wear her "finisher" T-shirt to Thanksgiving dinner with the family.

Throughout our coaching process, I utilized Bandura's sources of self-efficacy to instill confidence and increase motivation. "What is the most challenging feat you have ever accomplished?" I asked her.

She said, "I have never been a big runner or athlete, so I don't know how to answer that question."

"It doesn't have to be something athletic," I explained.

"I was in the school musical my junior year," she said. I used this *prior accomplishment* to help her connect emotionally with an experience of success, and she told me it was a major commitment. "I had to practice every day for three months!" To keep up with her schoolwork and remain in the musical, she had to give up social media at night. "I had to get up early on the weekends to practice. That was really hard because I like to sleep on the weekends."

"Tell me about opening night," I said.

"I was so scared before I went on stage that I thought I was gonna throw up!" She described how she "channeled" her nervous energy into her performance and "nailed" every line. I watched her as she remembered this experience. Her eyes widened, and she smiled. "At the end of the play, we received a standing ovation, and I was presented with a bouquet of roses from my parents. It was the most exhilarating thing that ever happened to me!"

She was excited and fired up as she spoke to me. I seized this opportunity to engage her in an *imaginary experience* about her marathon goal. "Let's imagine you are at the start of the marathon. You have been practicing, making sacrifices, and getting up early, ready to go. You feel nervous, but you channel all that energy into your performance. See yourself running and 'nailing' it, mile after mile. At the finish line is a crowd of people giving you a standing ovation. You feel exhilarated as you cross the finish line!"

As we continued our discussion, I had her imagine barriers or roadblocks she might experience along the way. "When I get anxious, I start to doubt myself and sometimes find myself on the couch with a pint of ice cream and a bag of cookies, binging Netflix," she said.

I work to help her *manage emotions*. "What about the marathon makes you most anxious?"

"I feel like an imposter out there with all those skinny athletic people!"

"How do you think they felt before their first marathon?"

"They were probably a little scared themselves," she said.

"When a person is trying to learn something new, are they an imposter, or are they simply someone trying to learn something new?"

"Yeah, I know what you mean," she replied.

"Have you ever been to a marathon and watched runners cross the finish line?"

"Yes, I have," she said. "It was really cool."

"Was everyone who crossed the finish line skinny?"

"No," she responded. "I was surprised how many different body types crossed the line."

"Was everybody running across the finish line?"

"No, some people were walking."

"Were the people who ran across the finish line happier than the ones who didn't?"

"Actually, no," she said. She explained that the runners who walked across were just as happy—"if not happier."

From there, we planned for the next time she felt anxious and found herself headed for the couch. I instructed her to take some time alone to do some deep breathing and get herself grounded in her goal and motivation. As she meditates, she is to reflect: "This is a challenge I have always wanted to do for myself. It is not about how fast. I don't have to be better than everyone else, and I don't have to be skinny. If I must walk for parts of the run, it is okay. After all, this is my first one. I can think of my training in the same way. I don't have to be perfect, but I do have to be consistent with my workouts. If I have a bad day, where I am not feeling super motivated, I can shorten my workout, but I need to stay off the couch and put in some effort."

As a coach, and having been coached, I know how impactful it is to learn from someone you admire and feel you can relate to. I introduced her to a client I coached a few years ago, who ran her first marathon in five hours and ten minutes. She is now on her fourth marathon and recently ran one in four hours and thirty minutes. Working with mentors is a great opportunity for *vicarious learning*. My former client met with her and shared strategies she learned to be successful. She agreed to do some training runs with her and gave her feedback on how to improve. She introduced her to a running group at her local club. My client joined the group and reflected on how she became a "much better runner" by having support from "people who have been there." I often talk to my clients about this kind of learning as "feeling it in your bones." As I have learned more about neuroscience, I have become aware that "feeling it in your bones" is not so far from the truth!

In month four of her training, she mentioned that she felt tired, like she wanted to quit. "This is really time-consuming! I don't know about this. I'm not sure if I have what it takes!"

I engage her in a *verbal persuasion* dialogue. "Remember when you told me about getting a part in the high school play and 'nailing' the lines? Do you remember all the sacrifices you made: giving up electronics at night, waking up earlier on the weekends, and practicing your lines every day for three months?"

"I sure do," she replied.

"Do you remember taking a bow at the end of the performance?"

"I will never forget it."

"Can you see yourself taking a bow at the finish line of the marathon?"

"That would be so cool!" she exclaimed.

I reflect on my experience with her for the past four months. "I know you can do this! I admire your commitment and courage to challenge yourself by facing your fears and doing something you have never done! You are hardworking and tenacious! It has been an honor to witness this with you and watch you grow stronger every day! You've got this!"

In the story above, I shared several high-level coaching techniques. I strongly encourage you to apply them as you work with your child to achieve your desired goals. Below is an example of an academic goal for your child and strategies for success.

Step 1: Identify a goal and write it down.

Teen: Achieve a 3.5 grade point average.

Parent: Based on your knowledge of your child's ability and how they're functioning academically, assess whether this is a realistic goal.

Step 2: List tasks needed to obtain the goal.

Teen:

- I will maintain 90 percent attendance.
- If an absence occurs, I will commit to getting missed information from a peer or teacher.
- I will commit to using my instructor's office hours if I need support. Office hours are Wednesdays and Fridays from 3:30 to 5:30 p.m.
- I will commit to refraining from using social media while I am studying.
- I will spend two hours a week studying for each of my classes.
- I will commit to waking up no later than 11:00 a.m. on weekends to study.
- I will check in with my parents once per week to update my progress.

Parent:

- I will check in with my child every week to see how they're doing.
- I will create a structure of support and accountability for them to succeed.

Step 3: Start working on the tasks.

Teen:

- I will begin working on these tasks at the beginning of the fall semester on September 4.

Parent:

- I will commit to monitoring my child's progress.

Step 4: Add to tasks as needed.

Teen:

- If I discover something else is needed, I will add it to my task list.

Parent:

- I will continue to monitor progress, provide encouragement, and assist my child in adding tasks to their list if/when needed.

Step 5: Check off the tasks as they are completed.

Teen:

- I will keep a record of my tasks and check them off as I complete them.

Parent:

- I will take time to reflect on how my child is doing at completing tasks identified in step 2, to achieve the overall goal of a 3.5 grade point average.
- We will review the steps she/he took to complete the task.
- If obstacles were experienced along the way, we will discuss what was done to overcome them.

Step 6: When all tasks are complete, determine if the goal has been met.

Teen:

- At the end of the semester, I will evaluate my progress.

Parent:

- When my child comes toward the end of a goal period, I will reflect on their progress and provide constructive feedback.
- I will acknowledge and praise my child's hard work!

Chapter 10 Exercise:

Have a meeting with your child and orient them to this goal-setting process. As you guide your child through goal achievement, use coaching techniques to help them stay motivated and on track: prior accomplishments, vicarious learning, verbal persuasion, managing emotions, and imaginary experiences.

CHAPTER 11

Step—8: It's Not an Event, It's a Process

IF YOU ARE overwhelmed by all of the adversity our tweens and teens are facing, imagine how they feel. Time for a deep breath! Remember, just like my first-time marathon runner, you don't have to be perfect, but you do have to be committed to putting some effort in. Think of mental fitness not as a one-time event but rather as an ongoing process in which you are patient with yourself and your child along the way. Like anything, the more effort and persistence you put in, the easier it is and the more competent you become. In other words, it is a lifestyle.

All children deserve an opportunity to get into a position in life where they are doing what they were born to do. It is easy for us to feel like a failure when our kids are struggling. Struggling is normal. It's not only normal but necessary. Below is a story we use in family therapy to illustrate this point:

The struggle to become a butterfly: A true story (author unknown; edited)

A family in my neighborhood once brought in two cocoons that were just about to hatch. They watched as the first one began to open, and the butterfly inside squeezed very SLOWLY and PAINFULLY through a tiny hole that it chewed in one end of the cocoon. After lying exhausted for about ten minutes, following its AGONIZING emergence, the butterfly finally flew out the open window with its beautiful wings.

The family decided to help the second butterfly so it would not have to go through such an excruciating ordeal. So, as it began to emerge, they carefully sliced open the cocoon with a razor blade. The second butterfly never did sprout wings, and in about ten minutes, instead of flying away, it quietly died.

The family asked a biologist friend to explain what had happened. The scientist said that the difficult struggle to emerge from the small hole actually pushes liquids from deep inside the butterfly's cavity and into the tiny capillaries in the wings, where they harden to complete the healthy and beautiful adult butterfly.

Without the struggle, there are no wings!

So, you see, the struggle is a very important part of this process. You are not a failure. Your child is not a failure. You are both going through different stages of learning on the road to mental fitness. In the field of coaching, we often refer to a model that illustrates stages of competence when learning and trying new things.

Stage I—Unconscious incompetence. In this initial stage, we are misdirected in our efforts to help our kids succeed and are unaware of it, like Richard in chapter five, who was unable to connect the dots and see how his harsh disciplinary practices were harming his relationship with his child.

Stage II—Conscious incompetence. We are consciously aware that we are struggling to help our kids succeed. Upon reflection, in chapter nine, Amy's mother realized that what she had been doing to help her daughter was not working.

Stage III—Conscious competence: We are consciously aware that we are helping our child succeed. In chapter one, Tommy's parents learned that setting healthy boundaries and becoming true allies for his success was working. Tommy returned to the hockey team and agreed to refrain from chemical use during the season.

Stage IV—Unconscious competence. We have learned to help our kids so well that we don't have to think about it. Christopher's parents, in chapter seven, worked hard to integrate skills into their parenting and happily reported that they didn't have to nag him anymore. It just came naturally. It had become their lifestyle.

What would it be like to learn how to guide your child to mental fitness and success so well that it becomes as natural as breathing? One of my favorite client memories is a celebration I had with a mother and her daughter, with whom I had worked for quite some time. Mary had been struggling notoriously in school. In stage one, her mother was unaware that her yelling was undermining her daughter's progress. In stage two, her mother became aware that yelling and punishment were not helping. With this new awareness, she moved into stage three, and we were able to work through all kinds of distractions and teen stressors. Her mother hung in like a trooper. It wasn't easy at first, but as time went on, she reached stage four and found herself applying her skills naturally, no longer needing my help. A few years later, I got a phone call from Mom, ecstatic about receiving news that her daughter had been accepted into the University of Minnesota. We had a party in my office. Mom's life opened up as well—"I have more time for self-care, and now we are thinking about doing some traveling." She cheerfully reported that her relationship with her husband had improved due to much less stress in the house.

Parents, I wish you well on your journey to mental fitness with your child and unconscious competence. You have demonstrated your commitment. You've got this! Remember your skills, breathe, and trust the process.

CHAPTER 12

Conclusion

"If I could give my teenager three things, it would be the confidence to always know their self-worth, the strength to chase their dreams, and the ability to know how truly, deeply loved they are." —Unknown

BY NATURE, TEEN years can be quite turbulent as our kids are growing, developing, and seeking to discover who they are. The process I have outlined is easy to follow. However, as previously stated, it takes commitment and stick-to-itiveness. In chapter one, I highlighted the importance of getting started on the mental fitness process as soon as possible. In chapter two, I shared stories of my struggles and how I solved my problems. Chapter three underscores the importance of foundational and emotional intelligence skills. In chapter four, we did some exploration to help you become clear not only about concerns for your child but also your hopes and dreams for them. In chapter five, I provided several examples of parenting styles and encouraged you to examine the connection between how you were parented and how you are currently parenting your child. In chapter six, I discussed pressing problems unique to internet-generation kids, such as electronics and social media, bullying, loneliness, the vaping epidemic, peer pressure, teen suicide, COVID-19, racial consciousness, sexuality and gender identity, and the sharp increase in depression and anxiety. Chapter seven was about learning how to clean the slate with your child to design a strong working alliance as you move into the mental fitness process. In chapter eight, I reviewed foundational skills of time and money management, sleep hygiene, nutrition, and physical activity to help you create sustainable structures with your child to keep them on track. In the heart of the book, chapter nine, I explained the importance of infusing self-awareness, social skills, and empathy to help your child achieve and maintain mental fitness. Chapter ten taught you skills for building confidence and gave you a template for setting goals. In chapter eleven, I introduced you to stages of competence commonly used in the coaching world.

In reading this book, I hope you feel optimistic and are armed with tools and strategies to help your child strengthen mental fitness. Remember, it is okay to ask for help. *Psychology Today* is a great online resource for finding therapists and life coaching in your area. School counselors are also a good resource for assessing and referring for specific services. It has been an honor to be on this journey with you, and if I can assist you in any way, please feel free to reach out.

https://davidhoy.com/

ACKNOWLEDGMENTS

THIS BOOK IS a culmination of five years of research and decades of personal experience working with families and children. Thanks once again to MarDee Rosen Hall, my friend, colleague, and contributing editor, who inspired me to keep going and drill down to make the stories in this book fun, interesting, and informative. As clinical director and a lead administrator at David Hoy & Associates for twenty-five years, she has always kept us grounded in our mission to serve. She is a blessing to everyone she encounters.

As always, thanks to my wife, Sandy, our CFO and controller at David Hoy & Associates, for her business acumen and humanistic approach to leadership. I couldn't have a better partner in life or at work, and I am eternally grateful.

Thanks to lead administrators Kathy Wolfbauer and Nicole Recke for their hard work and compassion for employees and clients as they tackle the details that make us run smoothly.

REFERENCES

Abraham Maslow, Theory of Human Motivation, In R. J. Lowry, RJ., Ed., Dominance, Self-Esteem, and Self-Actualization (Germinal papers of A. H. Maslow, Brooks/Cole, Pacific Grove pp. 157-173, 1973, Belmont, CA: Wadsworth)

Albert Bandura, Self-efficacy: Toward a Unifying Theory of Behavioral Change, (Psychological Review, 1977), 84, 191-215. doi:10.1037/0033-295X.84.2.191

Albert Bandura, Social Foundations of Thought and Action: A Social Cognitive Approach. (Englewood Cliffs, NJ: Prentice Hall, 1986).

American Psychological Association, (Stress in America Survey, 2022), Retrieved from: https://www.apa.org/news/press/releases/stress

Ana Sandoiu, Teens Get as Much Exercise As 60-Year-Olds, Study Shows (Medical News Today, 6/19/2017), Retrieved from: https://www.medicalnewstoday.com/articles/317975.php

Angella Duckworth, Jamie L. Taxer, Lauren Eskreis-Winkler, Brian M. Galla, James J. Gross,

Self-Control, and Academic Achievement, (Annual Review of Clinical Psychology, Vol. 70:373-399 (Volume publication date January 2019), Retrieved from: https://www.annualreviews.org/doi/abs/10.1146/annurev-psych-010418-103230

Ashley Abramson, Children's Mental Health Is in Crisis, (Monitor on Psychology, 1/1/2022), Vol. 53 No. 1., Retrieved from: https://www.apa.org/monitor/2022/01/special-childrens-mental-health

CBS News Los Angeles, 25 Is The New 18? Study Says Teens Are Growing Up Slower, September 19, 2017/11: AM KCAL News, Retrieved from: https://www.cbsnews.com/losangeles/news/teens-growing-up-slower/

Centers For Disease Control and Prevention, Mental Health Among

Adolescents, (CDC Fact Sheet, 2009-2019) Retrieved from: https://www.cdc.gov/nchhstp/newsroom/docs/factsheets/dash-mental-health.pdf

Center for Disease Control and Prevention, Childhood Obesity in the United States, (2017-2020), Retrieved from: https://www.cdc.gov/obesity/data/childhood.html

Center for Disease Control, US Suicide Rates % Change: Comparison of Most Digitally Connected Generation, (CDC data, 2000-2016)

Center for Generational Kinetics, An Intro to Generations, (2016), Retrieved from: https://genhq.com/faq-info-about-generations/

Dan Buettner, The Blue Zones of Happiness: Lessons from The World's Happiest People (Washington, D.C., National Geographic, 2017)

Daniel Goleman, Emotional Intelligence: Why it Can Matter More Than IQ, (New York: Bantam Books, 1995, 6th ed)

Daniel Goleman, Social Intelligence: The New Science of Human Relationships, (New York: Bantam Books, 2006)

Dan Siegal, The Pruning Process in the Adolescent Brain; Video, (Kids in the House: The Ultimate Parenting Resource, 2023), Retrieved from:

https://www.kidsinthehouse.com/teenager/health-and-development/brain-development/pruning-process-adolescent-brain

Diana Baumrind, Diana Baumrind's 3 Parenting Styles: Get a Full Understanding of the 3 Archetypal Parents, (Positive -Parenting-Ally.com, 2017), Retrieved from: https://www.positive-parenting-ally.com/3-parenting-styles.html

Embrace Race with Moms Rising, Ten Tips for Teaching and Talking to Kids about Race, (2023), Retrieved from: https://www.embracerace.org/resources/teaching-and-talking-to-kids

Emily Guarnatta, How to Talk to Your Kids About Sex: An Age-by-Age Guide, (Choosing Therapy 2021), Retrieved from: https://www.

choosingtherapy.com/talk-to-kids-about-sex/

Emily P. Kingsley, Welcome to Holland, (1987), Retrieved from: https://www.emilyperlkingsley.com/welcome-to-holland

Eva Oberlie, Joseph A, Durlak, Rebecca D. Taylor, Roger P. Weissberg, Promoting Positive Youth Development Through School-Based Social and Emotional Learning Interventions: A Meta-Analysis of Follow-up Effects. (Society for Research in Child Development, 2017), Retrieved from: https://casel.org/2017-meta-analysis/

Gene Beresin, 7 Ways to Support Kids and Teens Through the Coronavirus Pandemic (The Clay Center for Young Healthy Minds, 2021), Retrieved from: https://www.mghclaycenter.org/hot-topics/7-ways-to-support-kids-and-teens-through-the-coronavirus-pandemic/

NBC Universal, About 40 percent of U.S. Adults are Obese, Government Survey Finds, Retrieved from: https://www.nbcnews.com/health/health-news/about-40-percent-us-adults-are-obese-government-survey-finds-n1144091

Ibram X Kendi, How to Raise an Antiracist Baby, (Random House Books, 2022)

Jean Twenge, Teens Have Less Face Time Their Friends-and are Lonelier Than Ever (The Conversation, updated, 7/27/2022), Retrieved from: https://theconversation.com/teens-have-less-face-time-with-their-friends-and-are-lonelier-than-ever-113240

Jean Twenge, iGen: Why today's super-connected kids are growing up less rebellious, more tolerant, less happy-- and completely unprepared for adulthood (and what this means for the rest of us), (First Atria Books hardcover edition, 2017). New York, NY: Atria Books.

Jennifer Harvey, Raising White Kids, (ARBINGDON PRESS NASHVILLE, 2017)

John Oliver, Trans Rights II: Last Week Tonight with John Oliver, Retrieved from: https://www.youtube.com/watch?v=Ns8NvPPHX5Y

Kathleen Smith, Common Triggers of Teen Stress (Psycom, Updated October, 2022), Retrieved from: https://www.psycom.net/common-triggers-teen-stress/

Korn Ferry, The Plant Based Future of Food, (Korn Ferry Perspectives, 2020), Retrieved from: https://www.kornferry.com/content/dam/kornferry/docs/perspectives/perspectives-plant-based-future-of-food.pdf

Mitch Berger, One-Third of First-Year College Students Report Mental Health Issues, (Healthline Media, 2018), Retrieved from: https://www.healthline.com/health-news/college-frosh-mental-health

Mitch Zeller, Youth E-cigarette Use Remains a Serious Public Health Concern Amid the Pandemic, (US Food and Drug Administration, 9/30/2021), Retrieved from: https://content.govdelivery.com/accounts/USFDA/bulletins/2f55a59

Newport Academy, The Scary Truth Behind Teen Eating Disorders: Causes, Effects and Statistics, (2017), Retrieved from: https://www.newportacademy.com/resources/mental-health/scary-truth-teen-eating-disorders/

Nicholas Bakalar, How Much Junk Food Do Teenagers Eat? (*New York Times*, 2015), Retrieved from: https://www.nytimes.com/2015/09/22/health/how-much-junk-food-do-teenagers-eat.html

PA Parent and Family Alliance, What to Do as Soon as Your Child Comes Out to You. (2023), Retrieved from: https://www.paparentandfamilyalliance.org/lgbtqiatipsheet

Pew Research Center, Cell Phone Ownership, Overall Cell Ownership Steady Since 2009, (3/19/2012), Retrieved from: https://www.pewresearch.org/internet/2012/03/19/cell-phone-ownership/

Rachel M. Cautero, A Parents' Guide to Teaching Teens About Money. (Parents, Dotdash Meredith Publishing Family, 3/24/2021), Retrieved from: https://www.parents.com/kids/teens/make-money/a-parents-guide-to-teaching-teens-about-money/

Rebecca T. Leeb, Rebecca H. Bitsko, Lakshmi Radhakrishnan, Pedro Martinez, Rashid Njai, Kristin M. Holland, Mental Health-Related Emergency Department Visits Among Children <18 Years During the COVID-19 Pandemic-United States, January 1-October 17, 2020, (Centers For Disease Control, Morbidity and Mortality Weekly Report, Weekly / November 13, 2020 / 69(45);1675–1680https://www.htm), Retrieved from: https://www.cdc.gov/mmwr/volumes/69/wr/mm6945a3.htm#suggestedcitation

Richard Harris, Got Water, Most Kids, Teens Don't Drink Enough, (MPR news, 2015), Retrieved from: https://www.npr.org/sections/health-shots/2015/06/11/413674246/got-water-most-kids-teens-dont-drink-enough

Rob Stein, The Surgeon General Warns Youth Vaping Is Now An 'Epidemic.' (NPR news, 2018), Retrieved from: https://www.npr.org/sections/health-shots/2018/12/18/677755266/surgeon-general-warns-youth-vaping-is-now-an-epidemic

Ruthann Richter, Among Teens, Sleep Deprivation an Epidemic, (Stanford Medicine News Center, 2015), Retrieved from: https://med.stanford.edu/news/all-news/2015/10/among-teens-sleep-deprivation-an-epidemic.html

Staff Writer, Can Exercise Boost Your GPA?, (California College of San Diego, 2018), Retrieved from: https://www.cc-sd.edu/blog/can-exercise-boost-your-gpa-https:www.verywellhealth.com/how-much-exercise-does-your-teen-really-need-2611242

Scottie Andrew, More US Adults Identify as LGBTQ Now Than at Any Time In The Past Decade, a New Poll Says, (CNN; updated

2;36 PM EST, 2/17/2022), Retrieved from: https://www.cnn.com/2022/02/17/us/lgbtq-population-increase-gallup-cec/index.html

The Associated Press, Floyd's Death Laid Bare the Minnesota Paradox of Racism, (May 24th, 2021), Retrieved from: https://www.mprnews.org/story/2021/05/24/floyds-death-laid-bare-the-minnesota-paradox-of-racism

The Trevor Project, Facts About LGBTQ Youth Suicide (12/15/2021), Retrieved from:

https://www.thetrevorproject.org/resources/article/facts-about-lgbtq-youth-suicide/

US Food and Drug Administration, Youth E-cigarette Use Remains Serious Public Health Concern Amid COVID-19 Pandemic, (9/30/2022), Retrieved from: https://content.govdelivery.com/accounts/USFDA/bulletins/2f55a59

Washington Post, USDA Replaces Food Pyramid With 'My Plate' In Hopes To Promote Healthier Eating, (2011), Retrieved from: https://www.washingtonpost.com/national/usda-replaces-food-pyramid-with-myplate-in-hopes-to-promote-healthier-eating/2011/06/02/AGRE16HH_story.html

William Sears, Breakfasts to Improve Performance at School/Work (Wellness Institute, 2019), Retrieved from: https://www.askdrsears.com/topics/feeding-eating/family-nutrition/brain-foods/brainy-breakfasts-improve-school-and-work-performance

www.ingramcontent.com/pod-product-compliance
Lightning Source LLC
LaVergne TN
LVHW041814060526
838201LV00046B/1270